OVERCOMING LIFE'S
CHALLENGES WITH
SASS AND STYLE

MOANA ROBINSON

First published by Ultimate World Publishing 2022
Copyright © 2022 Moana Robinson

ISBN

Paperback: 978-1-922828-38-5
Ebook: 978-1-922828-39-2

Moana Robinson has asserted her rights under the Copyright, Designs and Patents Act 1988 to be identified as the author of this work. The information in this book is based on the author's experiences and opinions. The publisher specifically disclaims responsibility for any adverse consequences which may result from use of the information contained herein. Permission to use information has been sought by the author. Any breaches will be rectified in further editions of the book.

All rights reserved. No part of this publication may be reproduced, stored in or introduced into a retrieval system, or transmitted in any form, or by any means (electronic, mechanical, photocopying, recording or otherwise) without the prior written permission of the author. Any person who does any unauthorised act in relation to this publication may be liable to criminal prosecution and civil claims for damages. Enquiries should be made through the publisher.

Cover design: Ultimate World Publishing
Photography: Sumico Photography
Layout and typesetting: Ultimate World Publishing
Editor: Isabelle Russell

Ultimate World Publishing
Diamond Creek,
Victoria Australia 3089
www.writeabook.com.au

DEDICATION

For my daughters, Dayna and Molly, and my grandchildren, Adam, Lucas, Charlie, Jeremy, Kieran and Taylor.

FOREWORD

As a hospital chaplain, I meet many interesting people. Sadly, many of them are experiencing vulnerable and challenging times in their lives.

That was how I met Moana. Although Moana had been and was continuing to navigate ongoing health issues, she had something special about her that stood out. Her resilience and her goodness shone like a bright beacon within and around her.

Regardless of who we are, in our lives we often find ourselves caring for others, either formally or informally. Often, we don't realise the difference we can make, both positively and negatively, through our encounters with others. But when one cares on a professional level through teaching, guiding and /or mentoring, the load of having to be strong and able to handle anything all the time can be overwhelming. That in itself can be debilitating and destructive, and so the question arises, "Who cares for the carer?"

The caregiver can surprise us sometimes, being a family member, friend, stranger or pet.

I hope you find something in this book that will speak to you and that you will get to know Moana and Teddy through their story and learn from their shared lived experience.

Chaplain Petra
Hospital Chaplain

CONTENTS

Dedication	iii
Foreword	v
Introduction	ix
The Start of a Whole New World	1

PART 1 — 9
1. Teddy's Revenge — 11
2. Expect the Unexpected — 21
3. Trust and Vulnerability — 31
4. Light at the End of the Tunnel — 35
5. Resilience and Choices — 43

PART 2 — 51
6. The Strategy — 53
7. Life Lessons — 65
8. Look Backward to See Forward — 71
9. Teddy's Tips — 77
10. Life Tools And Gifts — 85

Afterword	93
Appendix	95
Acknowledgements	97
About the Author	99
Speaker Bio	101

INTRODUCTION

Let me introduce to you Teddy James Robinson, the little guy who changed my life. We named him Teddy James, as he was born on the same date as our eldest grandson, Adam, whose middle name is James. James was also my father's first name.

To get our story started, let me give you a bit of background of how our special little canine friend, Teddy the Cavoodle, joined the family. Teddy James Robinson, Teddy, Mr Ted – and many more nicknames to come. As our story unfolds, you will see the importance of sharing

Teddy's Revenge

Teddy's tale with you, why Mr Ted is the protagonist of this story and just how he changed my life. Teddy has a personality that I didn't ever think of a dog having. He is very intelligent. His dad is a Toy Poodle and his mum is a Cavoodle (which is part Cavalier King Charles Spaniel and part Poodle). He learned very quickly as a puppy and helped me in a very unusual way to get through a very scary time in my life. It is all about putting things in perspective and realising that how you think about a situation determines the result.

I hope you enjoy and benefit from this book, as there will be big and small events in life to challenge and test everyone. I recommend highlighting any parts in this book that you would like to remember – holding a physical book in your hand is good (as it strengthens our connection to what we are reading and absorbing), and dog-eared pages are even better.

In 2021, I came scarily close to death. This experience had a profound effect on my perspective on what is important in life. Several times in one week, I was brought back from the brink of death. Within just a few months, I had seven surgeries — four in the same week. Three of those were emergencies. I spent that whole week in intensive care. The parade of challenges was relentless, and the experiences caused me to reflect on many aspects of life, including what makes us resilient when challenges come our way.

I had already developed a huge reservoir of inner strength that I didn't know I had. Since then, I have discovered the key factors that have made me more resilient than ever. We live in a world where there will always be unforeseen events and challenges to our emotional and physical strength. I hope that by sharing my story with you, you will be able to develop your own resilience to prepare you for whatever comes your way in life.

With the benefit of hindsight, I can see now that prior events prepared me. Those events really rocked me to the core. I developed resilient practices by studying coaching, reading personal development books

Introduction

and creating the habit of taking one day at a time. That's how I got through the life-threatening battles that I came up against in 2021.

Thanks to Teddy, I was given a new way to look at all of those events. Teddy brings us joy and makes us laugh when he listens intently to what we are saying with such a wise expression on his face, cocking his head from side to side. He always brings his favourite toy, Bunny, and drops it not quite within reach, while staring intently at you with his big brown eyes. The minute he thinks you are going to grab Bunny, he plonks his paw on it — hard. The goal is to have a tug of war or chase him for Bunny. If he wants to play and you ignore him he will get his other favourite, Chicken, one of those ugly squeaky stretched-out rubber chickens. He will keep tapping you on the leg with Chicken until you play with him. The highlight of my day is waking up to see Teddy and hearing the funny noise he makes when he yawns.

Teddy is such a joy to be with and has provided a great bond for my husband and I. While writing this book, I have been able to gain perspective on what makes me resilient. I see now that you, too, can rewrite the story of your life simply by looking at it in a different way. Lightness can replace heaviness, just as humour can replace the most serious of issues. Teddy gave me a reason to smile through the healing and gave me the ability to have a more optimistic view on life. Before Teddy and this story, I knew the right way to think and the choices to make. However, I was not fully doing this. Rather, I was simply going through the motions.

Life is so unpredictable, and if we are staying safe wrapped up in cotton wool, we are not truly living. I believe that I am a stronger person than I was ten years ago, as well as much wiser and aware of how to deal with the unexpected day-to-day events that can arise.

I realise that many people experience terrible calamities in their lives. The events I have experienced may seem insignificant compared to what others have been through. So, I have created this book as a light-hearted legacy. I want it to be a reminder so that if any of us experience any of life's major calamities, we may learn as I have that taking each day at a time and taking one step at time with a positive and determined attitude is what gets you through.

Teddy's Revenge is a metaphor for unexpected events. I am sure there will be many more events in my lifetime and in yours that can challenge, frustrate, devastate us and shake us up. Within the space of the two years, I was writing this book, the topical news events have been bushfires, the pandemic, wars and floods. We can learn from these challenges for a wiser and more understanding present and future. What seems like relentless torrents of events can be blessings in disguise. *Teddy's Revenge* is my way of sharing the strategy that I have used to move on from times that could otherwise be lodged in my mind as negative events. Having Teddy in our lives and the cumulative effect of the significant experiences we have endured over the years have developed that resilience muscle which made me tough inside. It has been quite the journey.

This is the story of that journey.

THE START OF A WHOLE NEW WORLD

The Hottest January

When COVID hit at the beginning of 2020, we had no idea this would be the year of such massive global change. In Australia, where I live, the pandemic followed the devastating 2019-2020 Australian bush fires. Though the closest was over 60 kilometres away, the devastation was shown in news images of 186,000 square kilometres ablaze, nearly six thousand buildings lost, and nearly half of them homes. Thirty-four people died, including nine firefighters, as well as billions of animals. Every day for 79 days, my country felt the urgency and danger around us. The bush fires in March 2020 burnt an estimated 18.6 million hectares (46 million acres; 186,000 square kilometres; 72,000 square miles), destroyed over 5,900 buildings (including 2,779 homes). It was so terrible. The news was constantly on everyone's mind and the whole nation felt for those affected.

Staying Positive

Before the bush fires, my first book, *B Styled for Life – Living with Sass and Style Over 50*, was published in December 2019, which was all about colour and style. I was planning a book launch for early

2020, but I really didn't want to hold it because I didn't feel that I should be celebrating when so many people were experiencing loss and devastation. I know that many people felt the same way about holding their events and celebrating anything in their lives at a time like this. After much deliberation, I made the decision to go ahead with the book launch. It was important for morale for everyone to see positive happy events going on. I asked everyone invited to wear blue to 'cool' things down and show support. I was hoping the cool energy would get through.

I decided to donate a portion of the proceeds from the book launch to the Red Cross, the organisation helping with the bush fires. To address any concerns about whether donations made it to victims, I set up an official donation fund. That way, people would know that when they purchased my book, the money was going to the right place.

That night, I did feel proud and excited. I had written the book over the span of four months, and it felt like a real achievement. The book launch kept me busy. I had arranged for my friend, Jan Cranitch, who is a wonderful chef, to cater the event. Another friend, Janeen Vosper, agreed to be master of ceremonies and helped me prepare PowerPoint slides. It felt good to know I had an emcee so I could focus on talking about the book. My friend, Tina Litte, took registrations and helped with book sales along with Michelle Sleight, a fellow author. Family, friends and clients came along to support me. Also featured on the program were my artist friend and client Tracie Eaton, and other clients. A coaching friend, Andrew Low, who had written the foreword, helped with technological logistics. My younger daughter, Molly, gave me a necklace with my B Styled business name. My whole family was there. I only wished my mum could have come from New Zealand. She had read my draft and had been so supportive. I felt appreciated and loved.

That day was one of the hottest January days on record. I remember standing in front of the audience during my presentation as sweat ran down the back of my legs. I could literally feel it trickling down my legs constantly. Even the air conditioning was struggling to cope. We opened the doors, and people listened from outside on the landing.

Then the whole world changed.

Snippets of What Was to Come

One day, I was walking back to the car after a great gym session when Peter, my husband, phoned. He was away at the time and had been staying at a bed and breakfast place interstate. Over breakfast, he spoke to a young woman who was a scientist in the food industry. She was working in the area and had heard about something which was going to be huge news shortly. A virus had started in China and it was going to cause a lot of problems. She told him not to purchase any food from overseas and to be very careful about what we were eating.

This was at the very start of the COVID-19 outbreak. This would have been just something this young scientist and heard and maybe thought it was related to food as her job was something to do with hygiene of food in stores. Little did we know at the time just how big the whole coronavirus outbreak was going to get. It was the biggest and most far-reaching event I had ever heard of in human history to date. This is what is happening now at the current time while I am writing this book. I believe that many events in my personal world from previous years have equipped me for these times.

The First Thoughts

It was during the time of this coronavirus outbreak in 2020 that I started looking for a puppy. I wasn't the only person looking as many people had started working from home. Both of our daughters and their husbands have had three children each and have busy family lives of their own. I missed seeing as much of our grandchildren since moving to the coast. Our youngest grandson was turning five and we no longer had babies to cuddle. The children are wonderful and I love them so much, however I wanted to have that feeling of caring for and nurturing someone again. I know now what people mean when they call dogs their 'fur babies.' I started to notice dogs more and wondered whether we could have a little one living with us in our apartment. I knew that dogs made great companions and my dog-owning friends really enjoy having that companionship.. I had met some dogs with great personalities and my heart went out to them. I loved the way they looked at you and play with such enjoyment. I kept showing my husband photos of cute puppies and dogs. His response was, 'Hmm, yes. Cute.' This went on for a few weeks. I kept reminding my husband, 'Travel restrictions will keep us home for a while. When we do travel on our road trips, a small dog could come with us or we could easily find someone to dog-sit.' He observed that I was noticing dogs and puppies a lot. I saw a group of people having breakfast one day cuddling the most gorgeous puppy I had ever seen. I didn't know much about dog breeds. I said to my husband 'I'm going to ask what sort of puppy that is. He said, 'No, no, don't.' I did anyway. I went and spoke to the group and learned that it was a Cavoodle called Ivy, who is now one of Teddy's best friends.

Because my husband hadn't been that keen on getting a puppy, I didn't do anything more about it, apart from keeping my eye on animal shelter pages to see if there were any little dogs available, but I didn't discuss it further. Then, a month or so before my birthday, my husband and I were out to dinner and he said to me, 'I've been thinking. I don't know what to get you for your birthday. We can get a puppy if you like.' That was it. I was so excited. We discussed it in more detail that night and agreed that it would definitely need to be a small breed because we live in an apartment. I started looking in earnest and I knew that I wanted a Cavoodle. The response was always the same from the breeders, 'You can go on a waiting list because everyone is wanting dogs at the moment. You may get one next year.' I had been researching and learned awful stories about puppy farms and that it was good to go to a registered breeder.

Not a 'Dog Person'

As a child in New Zealand, we had guinea pigs, three cats and some birds, but I had never been a dog person. It wasn't that I disliked dogs; I just gravitated more toward cats, and used to like it when my cat, Tiger, slept on my bed when I was a child. I still love the rhythmic sound of cats purring.

I can remember being quite scared of dogs. I used to walk to primary school along a narrow path past a high wooden fence and prepare myself as two huge Afghan dogs would always jump up at the fence and bark. I used to find this quite frightening as they were huge dogs with long hair and seemed to know what time we were going to be walking past. I had never warmed to dogs since then. My brother had a dog called Sid after my mum and dad divorced, but I didn't really get to know him very well as my brother lived with my dad and I had left with my mum.

When I was 16, I met Peter, who was 18 at the time and had a Samoyed dog called Tasha, short for Natasha. I became really fond of her. This was my first proper introduction to being around a dog. I discovered that dogs can have really great personalities and Tasha was a beautiful dog, always smiling. She ended up being a comfort to Pete's mum in her old age. When Tasha passed away, Pete's mother got another Samoyed called Sammy. Pete originally hadn't been allowed to have a dog, so he brought Tasha home as a puppy and as a gift for his mum. I always thought that was pretty smart of him.

The only other times I have had much to do with dogs were when our two daughters married and left home. They each had dogs and I became fond of them also.

Molly, our youngest daughter, and her husband had a Labrador dog, Ruby, that they had to train in order to socialise her for Vision Australia. We used to mind Ruby in training some weekends as my husband really loved her too. Ruby was and is a gorgeous dog. Molly was sad to see Ruby go after the initial training and socialising period finished. However, Molly then started a family, and together with her husband, Nic, they now have three gorgeous little boys. When Ruby was in training in Melbourne, she barked at someone who was close to the trainer there which resulted in Ruby not being able to complete the rest of the training. Molly and her husband had signed a form with an option to buy Ruby from Vision Australia if she failed the training, so now Ruby is the family pet along with a black Staffy called Phoenix. Our other daughter, Dayna, lives on acreage and has had dogs also which I met as puppies. They were great company and security for Dayna and her young family as Dayna's husband is a firefighter and does shift work.

The Search Begins

Once we had made the decision to get a dog, I signed up to some waiting lists and prepared myself for a long wait. However, a couple of weeks after that dinner discussion with my husband, I was lucky enough to be contacted by a guy I had made an enquiry with who said that a woman had not been able to get a dog after all. He asked 'Would you like to come and have a look?' My heart leapt and I felt butterflies in my tummy. I went straight away that evening to have a look. The breeder was only about a 30-minute drive away. I walked into the lounge room where the mother dog was with all her puppies at the breeder's home. The breeder and his wife had their little baby daughter sitting there playing and laughing with the puppies, and pointed Teddy out to me, with his golden brown fur that was straighter than his brothers and sisters. He had no hesitation at all about waddling over to greet me. His tail was wagging so fast and my heart melted. I was able to cuddle him and fell instantly in love. I knew straight away that I wanted to call him Teddy because he looked just like my 60-year-old teddy bear that I still have now from when I was a child which had exactly the same colour fur and dark eyes.

The Start of a Whole New World

The Day Has Come

The day came when Teddy was old enough for us to collect. I could hardly wait. We were looking after our granddaughter's cat, Willow, at the time while the family was away for the weekend. When we brought Teddy home, he weighed under two kilograms and Willow was quite a bit bigger than him. She was fascinated by this energetic little puppy, but also not very happy with him disturbing her peaceful time. She would creep up to where he was waddling around and exploring and then jump away when he got too close. She didn't seem to know what to make of him at all. I bought a soft canvas crate for Teddy and had researched how to toilet train him by keeping him in the crate next to my bed, waking him up during the night to take him out to the training pad. Living in an apartment, we had to plan how we were going to arrange the places for him to go to the bathroom until he had all his vaccinations and was allowed to go outside. Until puppies have had all their vaccinations when they are about 12 weeks of age, they are not supposed to be near other dogs or touch the ground outdoors because of the risk of catching canine parvovirus, which they are susceptible to from the age of six weeks to six months. As with cats, all boarding kennels and catteries would insist on pets having up-to-date vaccinations prior to being taken in to be looked after. One of my friends gave me a cute 'Doggie Diary' so I could record all of Teddy's milestones and important information.

I was so excited to wake up every morning to Teddy making little whimpering noises in his crate. He didn't make any loud noises at all until he was a few months old. My heart did a little flip-flop when I went to get him from the crate and playpen where he slept at night. During toilet training, he kept me busy getting up at night, reminding me of when our two daughters were babies. I was constantly cleaning up after Teddy but eventually, he got the hang of things. It was so wonderful to have this playful, happy little dog exploring everything and getting into mischief. I felt this immense love for this little guy as did my husband, and we both do even more so each day. Teddy loved the routine of getting brushed every day and still does. At puppy preschool, I learned the work was more about training the owners and finding out about dog behaviour. One trainer said when puppies run around like crazy, it's called 'zooming.' This is so much fun to see. We have a long apartment and he loves zooming around the coffee table, around and around. He zooms from one end of the apartment to the other, up on the bed, down again and it is pretty hard to catch him. We have a patch of grass near the swimming pool of the apartment complex and he zooms around and around there. As a little puppy, Teddy had so much energy and would spend ages running around outside on that patch of green grass. We would let him play there after his walk to let out some more of his endless energy. He gave us a lot of laughter and brought so much playfulness into our life.

But this is so much more than a story about a cute little dog named Teddy. There were more life lessons ahead, and Teddy was about to teach me.

Part 1

1.
TEDDY'S REVENGE

April 2021

My body was aching and my muscles felt weak. It was 3 a.m. and I hadn't slept well again all night. I was coughing repeatedly, constantly clearing my throat. For two weeks, I'd had a constant tickle and raw feeling. The vaporiser I bought didn't seem to help. It felt like the coughing would never end. I'd just spent ten days in hospital, most of it in intensive care, with a tube down my throat. I'd been in and out of the operating theatre four times in seven days.

I have always been a light sleeper. People describe me as a 'type A' personality, a term coined by cardiologists Meyer Friedman and Ray Rosenman in the 1950s to describe someone who is work-obsessed and competitive. I wasn't sure I agreed with the last part, but I have always been a go-getter.

The Start of a Bad Habit

My 'type A' tendency started when both my daughters were babies, and I would get up at night to feed them. Later, I would use that habit of waking during the night to achieve something that I hadn't had time to do during the day because of work. As an example, when the girls were toddlers, and I was going to aerobics, one night I woke up and started sewing. I had Lycra fabric, and I cut out leggings and leotards using a pattern. I sewed up a gym outfit, then wore it to aerobics when I woke up after only a few hours of sleep.

Another time when we had moved to a new house, I organised a family reunion for Christmas Day. I couldn't sleep the night before. I had already organised all the food for the 20 people who were coming. In the middle of the night, I sewed myself a dress, plus two matching dresses for my daughters, who were about two and three years old. They wore their beautiful new matching dresses on Christmas Day.

It started to be that I would be pleased if I woke up because I could finish the book I hadn't had time to finish reading during the day. That was a bad habit to get into as it set a pattern that was very hard to break. I would tell my daughters to never get into that crazy habit as although you can handle broken sleep better when you are young, as you get older it breaks you and wreaks havoc on your health. Later, as a coach, and when I paid more attention to health and wellness as my daughters were growing up, I realised the importance of sleep and that insomnia probably contributed to the severe depression and anxiety I suffered for years.

Those earlier years flashed back in my mind and even though it was thirty-odd years ago that my children were young and I had insomnia it made me appreciate a good night's sleep and that is what I was craving right now after my time in hospital.

Thoughts about my nighttime sleeplessness were on my mind after that night of constant coughing. But I wasn't thinking about the shiny tiles in the apartment when I walked from the bedroom through the carpeted office and onto the tiles, which led past the fireplace into the kitchen where I could get a drink of water to ease my dry throat. This time, I walked fast to the kitchen. Unlike years ago, I was not pleased to be kept awake during the night. Suddenly, in a split second, I skidded, slipped and fell straight down smack-bang onto the hard tiles. It happened so unbelievably quickly that it took my breath away. I noticed a massive splash of liquid all around me. A puddle of wee courtesy of our seven-month-old puppy.

My nightie was saturated and excruciating pain coursed up my left arm. I hunched over and cried out, 'Ow ow ow!' I had never felt sudden pain quite like this before. I felt sick with it. I wanted to curl up into a ball. I couldn't escape the intensity of that feeling in my arm. A feeling of dread washed over me. Apart from the acute pain, the feeling of dread and 'inconvenience' was even more overwhelming. I felt frustrated with myself for not turning on the light or not having a water glass next to the bed. Those were my overarching thoughts. I berated myself.

My husband is usually a pretty heavy sleeper, but he must have heard me and he came out straight away. He got me to sit on the couch. He wrapped a tea towel around my arm and got some ice. I was still hunched over as if to cover the constant stab in my arm to soften that feeling. I felt like vomiting. I thought and said out loud over and over, 'I just don't need this,' and, 'I can't believe it.' What really worried me was now something else had happened. This was going to mean a 'fix-up' of sorts. Little did I know.

Right then and there, Teddy came out and quietly sat in front of me, not understanding what was happening. He tipped his head to one side. His puppy eyes looked at both us, questioning what was going on. His big black eyes looked so concerned.

Pete took a look at my arm. 'Don't look,' he said.

Pain and Decisions

I couldn't get away from the pain. It was relentless. My 'head brain' took over, and I focused on deciding what to do next. That seemed better to me than just giving in to the pain. I managed to get showered and changed even though it was difficult. 'What clothing could I wear that would not require me to move so much? Which emergency room would take care of me the fastest? This is what my brain decided to do. We chose the emergency room at the local private hospital as I reasoned that the ER at the Gold Coast Hospital would be too busy even during the early hours of the morning. I knew how huge Gold Coast University Hospital was having visited friends in there. It seemed so unbelievable that I was even thinking about hospitals again.

Years ago, I would have been a bit of an emotional wreck rather than such a logical thinker. Past experience, coaching training and learning to think more pragmatically played a part in how I dealt with this, I am sure. It was important to me that I sorted it out in the best way possible. Through the blur of pain, I remember thinking about the inconvenience and that it was another hold-up that I was going through in what I wanted to achieve. I used my phone to direct Pete as we drove to the local private hospital.

Arriving at the ER at 3 a.m., I was surprised to see so many people even at the smaller hospital at that hour. A woman sat across the way from me telling the doctor that she'd had a knee operation only a few weeks before. Then she had slipped over and broken the other knee. I was surrounded by all sorts of injured people. They all had such a variety of accidents. I was trying to focus on anything but my own body and what I was feeling. It was strange, but I almost had a sense of detachment. I also thought of Teddy at home and was wondering if he was okay. 'How long was this going to take?' My brain seemed to be going at 100 miles an hour trying to think of anything other than the agony. After what seemed like hours and hours, the doctor came in and saw me. He gave me a painkiller and sent me for an X-ray. I had to move my arm gently on the plate to get the different angles for the X-ray. On return to the ER, the doctor looked at the X-rays and said, 'Oh boy, you have made a mess here — you will need surgery. It's a real mess.' He told me that he would have to deaden my arm with an injection and then pull it out to manoeuvre the bones back into alignment. After that, he'd put on a cast to hold the bones in place until I could have surgery later that day. He said the radius and the ulna were both broken all the way through and that I would go onto the end of the day's operating list. He said it again. 'That is a *very* bad break!' I was devastated. A massive wave of fear flooded me. The last thing I wanted after having a month of surgeries previously was another general anaesthetic or to go into an operating theatre. I was literally shaking. My heart started beating extra fast and I felt sick.

They wheeled me off to a treatment room. Pete followed and sat on a chair. He covered his eyes as they gave me injections to deaden my left arm. The two doctors attending pulled the bones back into place and a cast was put onto my arm.

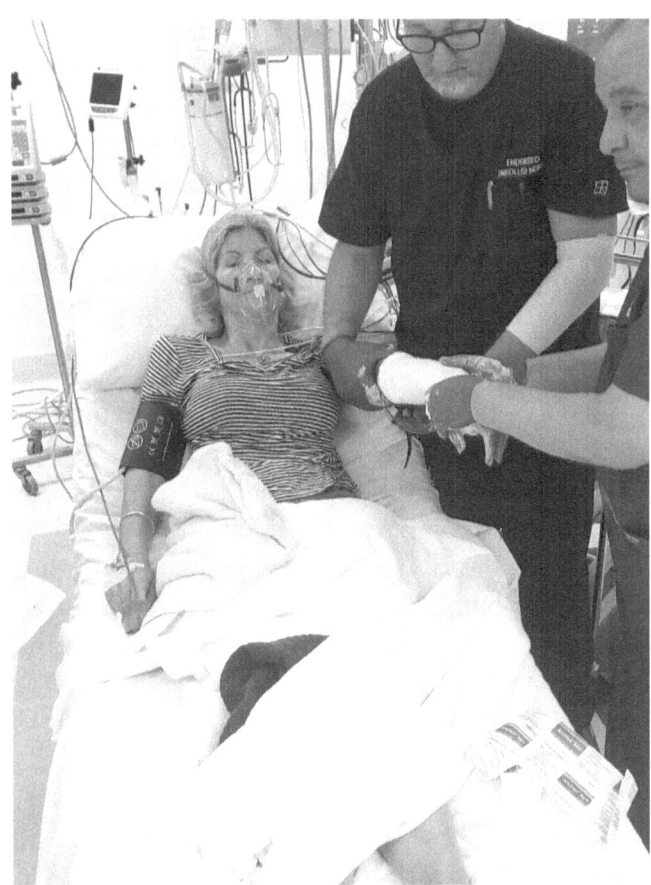

Despite the numbing medication, the first injection started to wear off that afternoon. By 6 p.m., I needed more painkillers. It got to the stage where I was actually looking forward to getting it fixed, and the operating theatre was looking more like a much better place to be. The drugs helped to dull the pain, but by the time they transferred me to a ward for the surgery, I was really feeling it and looking forward to getting this over with. Pete went home to check on Teddy. As I waited for surgery, the nurses told me I would be added onto the end of the surgeon's list for the day. They weren't sure what time that would be. Déjà vu, but relief from pain.

Finally, they got me ready for surgery. I showered with an antiseptic wash and changed into a hospital gown. It felt so much like *déjà vu* getting wheeled into a theatre. The anesthetist chatted to me, asking the usual identification questions. 'Please tell me your full name, date of birth and what you are in here for.' This would be about the twentieth time I had been asked these questions over the last few weeks. The anaesthetist commented on my hoarse voice. 'It's from multiple surgeries a few weeks before,' I said, and she suggested seeing an ear-nose-throat specialist. 'Your throat should have repaired by now,' she said. She also offered to give a nerve block injection in my armpit while I was under anaesthetic as this would completely numb the arm after surgery and allow me to get some sleep that night. I knew that I didn't want to spend the night in hospital but a good sleep sounded appealing. I agreed to this. 'A good night's sleep feels so important right now,' I said. I was trying to not think of the fact that I was having surgery again but rather envisioning being at home and sleeping in my own bed having this all over and done with. I woke up from surgery with what felt like a dead weight attached to me – it wasn't even a feeling of being attached. It was so weird. When changing out of the hospital gown, I picked up my left arm. It felt like a shop dummy's arm, but it was warm to the touch and *so* heavy. I wondered if this what it felt like for people who are paralysed.

The hospital staff said I could stay there overnight, but I was adamant that I wanted to go home. I was wheeled out to the car with a huge foam block called a Carter pillow. I had never seen these before. It looked like something homemade. It was a huge blue block of foam with a labyrinth of cutouts to feed your arm through so that it was always upright. I found out later these pillows are designed by a hand surgeon Peter R. Carter to reduce pain and swelling for post-fracture treatment as well as patients who have had mastectomies, dialysis or lymphodema.

I had a few days wearing the solid cast until I went to see the hand surgeon to have it removed and given a splint. Pete had to drive me to the hand clinic as I was out of action for driving for six weeks. I chose the hot pink splint with purple straps, something I found fascinating — you could choose your own splint colour. It was quite funny that I got excited about this, but hey, that is my business as a colour consultant. I really am just so passionate about colour. It was my chance to be a bit creative with something that I would be wearing constantly for six weeks.

They actually made the plastic removable splint at the clinic. I had always seen hand clinics and didn't realise how much is involved in getting rehabilitation for hand injuries. You really don't understand how much you use your hand and fingers until you lose the ability to manipulate them. It is like that with anything. A good lesson not to take anything at all for granted.

I used the big blue block (I nicknamed it my 'Lego brick') when sleeping, eating, anytime at all, really, as I was supposed to use it to keep my hand upright.

At the time this happened, I was completing a training course with Dent Key Person of Influence, and I was going to be writing a book. I had plans of writing another styling or business book as part of a book sprint. I was determined to finish the KPI Course.

Best Laid Plans

No matter how carefully a project is planned, something may still go wrong. That saying is adapted from a line in the poem *To a Mouse* by Robert Burns: 'The best-laid plans of mice and men often go awry.'

I was progressively losing my voice. No matter how much I rested, gargled or what I took to soothe my throat, it was getting worse and worse. I was typing with one hand and had the other hand upright in this blue block. I tried dictating the book, but that was not going to work with my voice the way it was. I made the decision to leave writing the next styling or business book until I had recovered fully

Unstoppable

I do believe in persevering and overcoming obstacles. This obstacle was one, though, that I realised I could not get around or over or through. It was a sign to me that now was not the right time to write the business book which was the final part of my course as I could not see a way to write it. I had committed to two styling and public speaking workshops, which had been postponed from the previous month due to the extended and unexpected turn of events. I did hold these workshops with my colleague, Janeen. There was one workshop in the city for an accounting practice. Janeen does the talk about public speaking and I do the styling part. The other was in my training room for some attendees who had booked in previously.

I had a very croaky and almost non-existent voice, and my arm was in a sling. Luckily, Janeen had experienced what I do with the colour drapes and we made it interactive. Janeen helped me hold the drapes while I held the other side with my good hand. I was able to make myself heard even with my croaky voice with the aid of the microphone.

I cringe when I think of how bad my voice sounded during that time. It was really awful, and I felt I had probably made it worse by persevering through it. I felt I had a commitment, though, to do the workshops, and I was determined to do them.

I did get three future bookings from the workshops, despite my voice and my arm. Luckily, the clients who booked were happy to wait for their consultations until I could drive again and my voice was back.

Wrist recovery took six weeks. During this time, my husband and I always jokingly referred to this whole incident as 'Teddy's Revenge.' He put up a post on Facebook about what had happened and everyone started referring to the incident as 'Teddy's Revenge'. It was so bizarre the way Teddy had left this great big puddle of wee next to the fireplace, which was the only way to get from the bedroom to the kitchen. After this happened, I always made sure that there was a bottle of water next to my bed in case I woke up during the night. I also turned the light on in case Teddy had any more 'wee surprises'. People who know about everything that happened have said, 'Wow, you couldn't write about it.' This expression is used to describe events or situations that are so unbelievable that they couldn't be written about or predicted beforehand.

Now, let's travel back in time to February and March to the series of unexpected incidents which tested my resilience.

2.
EXPECT THE UNEXPECTED

February 2021 – How It All Started

We woke up early, as we usually do. Pete offered to take my car down to work to wash it. I got up, had a shower and did some washing. Teddy really needed a wash so he had a shower too. He loved the water and always wanted to get into the shower when we were having one. Our shower is all on one level with no step up – it is just a walk-in with a curved tile wall. There is no glass at all so he would always run in and try to get wet. That morning, I just gave him his shower and dried him off with a hairdryer, which he was quite used to. As a six-month-old puppy, he loved playing, zooming around the apartment and going crazy with heaps of energy after his shower.

He also loved it when I was putting away the clean laundry so that he could see what he could nab out of the washing basket. Socks and undies are his favourite – our resident sock thief. He was such a fast runner, even more so now that he is older. He was running around and around while I was putting the clothes away.

I picked up the laundry basket full of folded clothes and stepped back, only to hear a sudden yelp from Teddy. But not just one little yelp. He kept on yelping and yelping. I was dismayed to see that he was holding up his paw. I could see that he had more than a fright. He was so tiny and helpless. My heart stopped, and I felt sick that I had caused him pain. I grabbed my phone off the dresser next to the bed and knelt down on the floor, frantically looking up the number for the emergency vet. I knew it would be too early for our usual vet to be open. I was shaking, I was so upset. Teddy snuggled next to me with his paw lifted. He seemed to huddle in close as though he knew I was getting help for him. He had stopped yelping and was pressing close to me, looking up at me while I spoke to the receptionist at the Animal Emergency Hospital. I then rang Pete to ask him to come home. 'I will be right there,' he said. We made it to the emergency vet, which felt like a long 20-minute drive. Ted was all bundled up in a blanket on my lap on the way to the vet. We had to leave Teddy there for X-rays. When we collected him that afternoon, I was dismayed to learn he had a broken leg. The emergency vets splinted his leg until we could see our usual vet for surgery. 'Is it okay if we take a photo of him for our social media?' they asked. They told me he had been the perfect patient. Looking back at the photo, it didn't even look like him as his fur looks so different to now.

Expect the Unexpected

We took Teddy in to see our vet early that week for surgery to have a plate put in his right front leg. Now we had to keep him confined for six weeks. He is such an energetic dog we didn't know how we were going to do this. He really was a good little guy, though. Teddy had to wear a cone around his head to stop him from scratching at his splint. I did something I never thought I would do – I bought him a doggy stroller so he could still go for walks around the block. Now I realise why so many people have them for their older dogs or dogs with injuries.

We took him for breaks outside. Because we live in a small village, a lot of people have dogs there and got to know Teddy because he is so friendly with other dogs and people. He used to bounce along on his back two legs like a bunny rabbit when he saw another dog or something he was excited about.

Of course, everyone asked what had happened to Teddy's leg when they saw him in the splint. I felt awful, even though the vet said it commonly happens. Because we saw the same people each day, once we had told the regulars what had happened, they didn't ask anything else about it. They just asked how he was going. I felt so bad about it every day. And even though people kept on saying to me, 'Accidents happen. It's one of those things' or, 'It's not the first time it's happened,' it didn't really help. I just felt bad every time.

Teddy, being such a good-natured little puppy was still happy. He was still quite playful. We had to stop him from jumping and keep him as quiet as possible. We took him for walks and collected the feathers that he loves. He could even spot them from the doggy pram and would lean over and bark until we stopped to pick them up. He looked like such a character with the feather in his mouth.

The stroller served its purpose, but we were so looking forward to the time when our frisky puppy could run around on his favourite grass patch again.

One afternoon, we took him to a beach near where we live. A group of children came up and asked if they could pat Teddy. They asked about the plastic cone on his head. One little boy burst out with, 'I know what that is! Our puppy had that so that he didn't lick his nuts!' We laughed as it sounded so funny coming from the little boy.

This whole time Teddy was recovering, I was so focused on him that it took my mind off the surgery I was scheduled for in a few weeks.

March 2021 – A Stroke of Luck

The surgery that loomed ahead was the result of a series of unexpected events that began one day at Pilates.

I love Pilates. Since we moved to the Gold Coast four years ago, my husband and I have been going to the same studio, where there are only six reformer beds. We go together three times a week. It is a beautiful relaxing atmosphere with pine floors, white walls and a hanging planter with trailing ivy. Essential oils waft through the air. The instructors and participants are lovely, and the equipment is great quality. The professional trainers always ask at the beginning of each class, 'How is your body today?' Going to Pilates has improved both my suppleness and mobility.

One morning at our usual 6 a.m. class halfway through the session I suddenly felt extremely dizzy. It wasn't just a little bit of light-headedness. It felt like I was going to black out as I was lying back on the reformer. It was an awful feeling that felt different to the vertigo I have previously experienced after long international plane flights. I went to sit up to do the next exercise and felt even worse. I said something like 'whoa' and held my head. It was unnerving. I sat up and got myself together. The instructor gave me some water, and I sat out the rest of the class.

That evening, as I was playing with Teddy, I felt that same sensation again. When it came a third time, I thought I should go to the GP. The doctor ordered blood tests and said I was extremely low in iron and I should get an iron infusion. He said this was something that couldn't be increased quickly through diet or supplements. I think the normal rating was 31 and I was down to about a 9. The doctor I saw advised me to have an infusion of vitamin B, which I went through with. The nurse administering the infusion promised that I would feel really good afterward but I really didn't feel any different. I felt quite well apart from the dizziness. I have since found out that I was so lucky to have had these dizzy spells as this was an indication of something more serious.

It Pays to Investigate

I still had more dizzy spells even after having this treatment. I went back to the GP and as a routine check he listened to my neck and he noticed something through his stethoscope called a 'bruit'. 'It's like a whooshing sound,' he said. 'Like the sound a washing machine would make.' He explained the blood was not getting from my heart to my brain on that side. He wanted to send me off to have an ultrasound. The ultrasound came back with a recommendation that I have an MRI. I had an MRI, and that came back with a recommendation that I should see a vascular surgeon. They found that I had over 95 per cent blockage in my right carotid artery. I didn't really understand what this meant, but the doctor told me it was very serious. He gave me a referral to get to see a surgeon as soon as possible. In the meantime, he said, 'If you have anything happen, if you have signs of a stroke, get to a hospital straight away.'

Asserting the Right to Choose

When I went to see the vascular surgeon on the Gold Coast, I left feeling uncomfortable with him. He seemed distracted and kept his earbuds in. He listened to my neck through a stethoscope and had to take his earbuds out to do this. I could hear the sound of someone speaking coming through the laptop computer that was open. He quickly rushed around and shut the laptop. This did not instil much confidence in me. The surgeon did agree that I had severe blockage of the carotid artery. 'It is up to you whether you have surgery,' he said. I left feeling very puzzled as to why my doctor was saying it was very serious, yet this surgeon seemed dismissive.

On the drive home, my husband commented to me, 'Did you realise he was listening to a podcast while he was talking to us?' I agreed. That's what I thought as well. That surgeon did say that I could get an MRI to check whether the dizzy spells had been mini-strokes as this would show up on the imaging. 'That would help you decide whether to get surgery or not,' he said. There was no way I wanted surgery, but I didn't want to have a stroke either. I contacted the surgeon's receptionist as the scan clinic wanted to know whether the MRI was to be with or without contrast dye. The message came back from him that without contrast would be fine. The MRI showed no signs that I had a mini-stroke. Great news! My GP had been insistent that I see a surgeon, however I did not feel comfortable seeing that particular surgeon again. A friend of mine had contacted me a few days prior to seeing the first surgeon, saying that if I wanted the name of someone good, she had a relative who had experienced a similar issue and he had seen a great surgeon. She gave me the name of the surgeon, and I thanked her. After the experience with the Gold Coast surgeon, I went to the GP and got another referral to see this other vascular surgeon in Brisbane. He was very easy to talk to. He explained everything in layman's terms and said that an over 95 per cent blockage was very serious. I asked him if it was possible for someone to still be okay if they only had one artery that was operating fully. 'A lot of people do go without or postpone surgery,' he said, 'but they almost always end up presenting at hospital with a stroke.'

Walking Time Bomb

That was enough for me. I did not want to walk around with the seconds ticking by, worrying that I could have a stroke at any time.

One of my aunts passed away from an aneurysm. Even though she was elderly, she was told that's what would happen, and it did. Her son also had an aneurysm causing his sudden death at age 54. I did not want to have something like that hanging over my head. I wanted to lead a full, fit and healthy life. After talking to the Brisbane surgeon, I felt happier about having surgery to correct this blockage and the artery. He said it would probably be a two-day stay in hospital. I had to sign something to say that there was a risk of death or stroke. I said to him, 'Well, if I have a stroke, I'll be in hospital anyway.' I felt confident going in for the surgery. I thought, 'This is just a hiccup. I will get it done and get it over with. Then I'll be back carrying on with my life.'

Sense of Trepidation

For some reason, in the days prior to the surgery date, I did feel a sense of trepidation. Being a life coach, I know how important it is to keep a positive mindset about these things. I have been part of several groups of coaches from all over the world. In one group in particular, I had been working to co-create a journey to share to the public called the Loving Your Life program. I am an mBIT coach, which stands for Multiple Brain Integration Techniques, and the Loving Your Life program is based on a book by Grant Soosalu, the co-developer of mBIT. I did a lot of balanced breathing to ease my anxiety about the surgery. I feel so grateful to the coaches with whom I was talking prior to surgery as I am sure that this connection as well as my own self-coaching journey helped me to cope with the trauma that was about to unfold.

We scheduled surgery for March 3, my sister's birthday.

An Unexpected Turn of Events

That morning, we were set with a plan to keep family and friends updated. A few of my friends knew that I had been having dizzy spells. I had told people that I was going into hospital for this carotid artery surgery. My husband had a list of a few people to ring or to let know once I had come out of surgery, which he did when I was out of the operating theatre and back on the ward. He contacted them straight away to say all was good and it was, until… Around 11 p.m. that night, when I was in the back in the ward, my neck started to swell and felt really strange. One of the nurses became concerned. She called the doctor on duty, and he called his colleagues, something they call a medical emergency team (MET). They were concerned as well. They made the decision to call the surgeon back in as I could hardly swallow or breathe through my mouth. The surgeon said I would need to go in for surgery again and made phone calls to quickly organise the operating theatre. I was feeling calm as I knew that I was in good hands and just wanted to get comfortable again as I could feel my neck swelling more and more. By this time, it was almost midnight. They had to call in the anaesthetist. The surgery would be an 'evacuation' to clear the swelling from my throat.

The surgeon explained to me that after performing the surgery they would insert a tube down my throat, and I would be unconscious and ventilated for about 18 hours. He said I would wake up in intensive care. I wasn't worried. I just wanted to be able to get the swelling to go down again. It all seems like a blur looking back, but I do remember waking up in a different part of the hospital. I've never been in intensive care before.

Watchful Eyes

I arrived at the Intensive Care Unit (ICU). I could see a nurse's station with a high stool behind it where a nurse was sitting making notes and watching the monitors behind me and on my left side.

Across the hallway, a man lay motionless with various machines attached to him. A nurse constantly sat at the end of his bed, watching him and making notes.

As I have found with intensive care, there's always a nurse sitting at the end of your bed at a desk watching you and the machines and making beeping noises constantly. I had all sorts of drips and connectors attached to me. I had a tube down my throat, and I had been out of it for maybe 12 or 18 hours. They sat me up and made me cough. I had to do some really big coughs while the tube was pulled from my throat. The nurses all wore plastic aprons. They were always putting those aprons on and throwing them away after. I discovered later the reason for this.

I spent the rest of that day in ICU dozing and reading a book a friend had loaned to me. It was a Nora Roberts book, and I remember thinking that it was nice to read a novel again. It was a mystery novel about a woman who trained dogs. I learned quite a bit about dogs when I was reading it. It made me think about Teddy and wonder what he was up to and whether he was managing with his splint. The funny thing was that I hadn't quite finished the book by the time I left hospital and read the last few pages at home — Mr Ted was a bit jealous of me reading the book and 'modified' (our name for anything Teddy chewed to bits) the cover of it. I later searched around the internet and found a replacement as I couldn't give it back to my friend Janine with a cover missing!

Not Again…

That night in intensive care, my throat started to swell. Doctors were called into ICU and by this stage, the surgeon who had done the original operation and had done the first evacuation was four hours away for the weekend because he thought everything had gone perfectly. He contacted another vascular surgeon to come in and see me. The other surgeon came in to see me and he said, 'I'm really sorry, but we're going to have to take you into the operating theatre again.' Again, I was wheeled into the operating theatre.

This time, I had a different anaesthetist. Same thing; I had to be intubated again. They asked me when I had last eaten. I had eaten a small meal that night as I was really hungry. This time when I came to quite a few hours later, and they pulled the tube out and I had to cough, it was a horrible experience because I vomited at the same time. Now I know why the nurses wore those plastic aprons. What a mess.

Intensity and Noise

I did not get any sleep due to the strong medication I was on. I was lying in bed constantly and getting injections in my stomach each day to prevent blood clots. I ended up being in intensive care for a whole week. The nurses would look outside the window and talk about the weather outside as I hadn't seen any natural daylight for the duration.

In the ICU, there were several instances where they had to revive patients. I could hear a lot of things going on during the night. I didn't realise what a noisy place intensive care was. I felt guilty because I was probably the healthiest person in that intensive care unit. The woman next to me almost died.

I heard the panic around me. I heard nurses and doctors being called. I heard families coming in. I heard a young woman crying. The next morning I did hear that woman in the bed next door talking to someone and she seemed to be okay. The nurse came in and asked me if I wanted a cup of tea, which felt crazy to me. All around me people were so ill. 'Is the woman next to me okay,' I asked the nurse. She replied, 'She's a very, very sick woman. She's not well at all.' The constant beeping noises, no sleep and concern for the people around me had worn me down. I was feeling very keen to move out of the ICU and out of hospital altogether. I really missed being at home. I missed Pete and cuddling Teddy. I desperately wanted to sleep. The next day, my younger daughter came to see me. I was so relieved and pleased to see her I burst into tears. It was so good to see her. We just hugged each other. Seeing Molly was like being visited by an angel.

3.
TRUST AND VULNERABILITY

Asking a Favour Made a Difference

My neck started to swell. I couldn't believe it. The same thing again! It was 9 p.m. and the doctor called other doctors into intensive care. They all stood around the edge of my bed, holding clipboards close to their chests and staring at me, without saying much at all. I didn't know what to do or say. We were just all looking at each other and my neck was swelling again, getting tighter and tighter.

Finally, I asked, 'What do you want me to do?' I felt like saying, 'You are the doctors.' It was then that I started to get really scared, really, really scared. I thought, When is this going to stop? When am I going to get out of here? I just want to be better.

The surgeon who had operated on me came to sit next to me. 'I'm going to ask you a favour.'

'What's that?' I asked.

'I want you to trust me.'

'Okay.'

'I'll be honest with you,' he said. 'I'm feeling paranoid because this has happened to you before. If we don't take you into operating theatre now I feel I'll be going home and then coming straight back again.' He continued, 'I'm not thinking of myself. I'm thinking of you going through all of this at midnight again.' He told me he was going to ask another vascular surgeon to come in and perform the surgery with him.

For some strange reason, I felt comforted by the fact that he was so open with me. I don't know whether it's because I'm a coach or whether one of my top values is honesty and integrity, but this surgeon was being vulnerable by telling me that he was feeling paranoid. That honesty was a huge comfort to me.

The way he spoke to me made a difference. He was asking me a favour, not just demanding straight away that I trust him. He didn't tell me that everything was going to be okay. He just was authentic and honest.

Groundhog Day

Off we went to the operating theatre. This time I was really scared. I couldn't stop shaking and shivering. I actually prayed to God. I knew I wanted to live. I really, truly, desperately wanted to live. This felt like a never-ending nightmare.I looked around the operating theatre, taking in everything that I could see, the doctors, the nurses, the shape of the room, where everything was, people talking and getting ready. It was as though all my senses were heightened. It was so weird because I had been in there three times before. Now, there were some of the same people and some people were different. The lights seemed brighter, the colours more vivid. The hospital green covers looked more turquoise and I noticed the different designs on the surgeons' caps. I noticed who was wearing glasses and who wasn't. Noises seemed extra loud. The clinking of equipment and the people talking even though they were talking in low voices about the procedures sounded noisy.

I was aware of everything all at once and felt like I was living though the film *Groundhog Day*. That may have been a comedy, but what I was experiencing was more like a horror movie. I just wanted to keep myself calm. I tried not to cry. I was talking to myself, remembering my calming techniques from coaching. I did some balanced breathing and kept myself as calm as possible. I was actually thinking of the people around me. I was thinking of the anaesthetist when he was putting the injection into my arm. This was the fourth anaesthetist I had met in one week. How awful it must be to put someone to sleep for surgery, especially when she signs the consent form while crying. One of my favourite sayings has always been that 'everyone has a choice.' In this instance, I knew that I didn't have a choice because I had to have this surgery or I would die. Afterwards, I wondered whether I had been overreacting. However, when I finally left intensive care a few days later and was back in the ward, one of the nurses told me they nearly lost me twice.

Breakdown Before Breakthrough

By this time, I was used to the procedure of having the tube taken out. I wasn't unconscious for as long during this surgery, but I was exhausted afterwards. When my husband called, it felt as though he was criticising me for being so amenable to the doctors when they advised that I needed to go back in. I knew, but he had not known at the time, that I didn't have a choice. I also didn't see a point in making things difficult for the surgeon by being upset or angry. During this conversation, I became upset. I realised he was questioning because he was concerned. I was frustrated because it seemed like he was saying I should have reacted in a different way when I felt I was only barely coping with each event as it came up. I was doing my best to keep myself on an even keel. The only way I knew was to remain calm and take each minute and hour as it came. I knew that I wanted the treadmill to stop. I didn't like someone, especially someone I loved, telling me that I should have reacted in a different way. I know it was my exhausted state, but I just started crying and couldn't stop. I felt bad because I knew that there were patients in that unit who were much worse off than me. It was unknown to me whether it would all happen again. I had run out any strength.

'Please don't cry,' my husband pleaded with me.

'I don't know how you are doing all of this. I couldn't go through what you are going through.'

A nurse came over and said, 'Don't cry, it's not good for you. You need to keep calm.'

That night proved to be the turning point.

4.
LIGHT AT THE END OF THE TUNNEL

Sitting Up At Last

I can't remember the exact order of events during my time in intensive care – just that one day I finally got to sit up and that felt great. A bubbly young physiotherapist showed excitement when I got to try out the brand new chair that had been delivered to intensive care.

There was a little plastic contraption given to me which looked like a kid's toy with coloured balls and clear plastic cylinders. To strengthen the lungs and airways again you had to blow through a tube and work at getting the balls to stay at the top of the tube for a certain length of time. If you have used these before, you will know that it is pretty much a challenge when you are feeling breathless after surgeries. When my husband or daughter came to visit, we laughed together as we could hear the person in the next bed doing the same thing and I was trying to make sure I kept working at it to keep the challenge going.

Every day, I received anti-blood clot injections in my stomach. Each night, it was hard to sleep. I didn't eat most of the time. One day, I looked down at my hands and hey didn't even look like mine anymore as I had lost so much weight. I looked and felt so old and tired, but I was so relieved to be alive.

I had been in that hospital bed for so long that I wasn't even sure what day it was. I vaguely understood I had missed a few events that I thought I was going to be home for. Normally I liked to read business or educational books, but instead, I got lost in novels, even though I was only reading a few pages at a time.

Tales From Teddy

Every day, my husband drove back and forth to the Coast. He would send photos to my phone of Teddy, still wearing his protection collar. I still felt sad when I saw the splint on his leg. In videos, I could see he was happy, though, wagging his tail and getting into mischief.

I still felt a twinge of guilt when I saw the plastic cone and the bandage on his leg. Pete managed to find more comfortable blow-up collar for Teddy, which turned out to be quite funny. Now, Teddy had a portable cushion around his head. Anytime he wanted to lie down, he would flop down, put his head on the cushion and go to sleep.

My Daughter the Truck Driver

My elder daughter, Dayna, had been driving a huge truck, which she drives for our car racing business as a parts supply vehicle. She had been to see me previously as well, driving from Melbourne to Sydney, catching a plane and coming straight to the hospital. When she came to the ICU, it was so good to see her. She had only just started driving the big truck. We joked that she would need to get a black singlet and some shorts and work boots. Dayna is an accountant and really enjoys driving the parts truck to the race meets. One night, she was going out to dinner somewhere but asked her husband to drop her at the hospital and spent a few hours with me, which was lovely. That meant a lot to me.

A Strange Familiarity

After the ninth day in intensive care, I was wheeled back to the ward. It felt strange and only vaguely familiar. The nurses welcomed me back. Three of them talked as though they had seen me before. I couldn't remember being there in the first place. It was quite an eerie feeling. The next day, I realised that a lot of the nurses' faces did seem quite familiar.

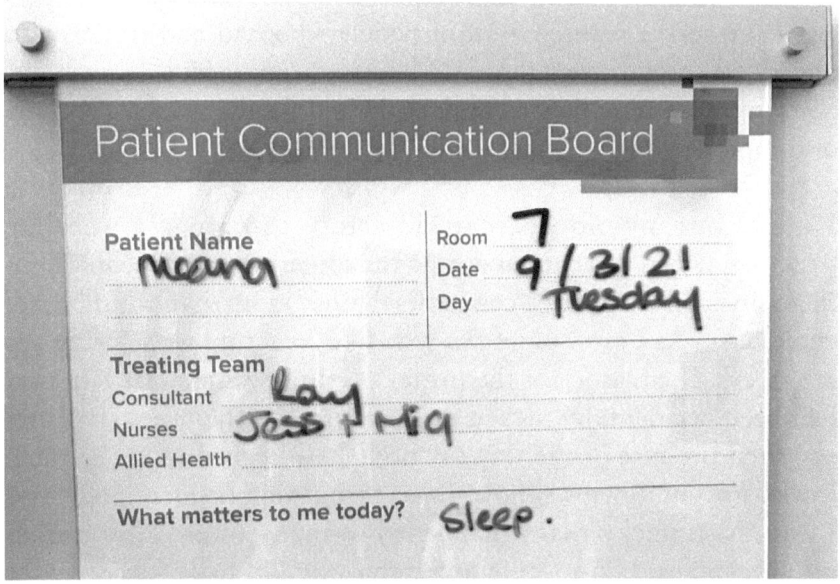

All the nurses kept saying I was a 'real trouper' or 'so strong.' Each time they changed the guard in ICU, the outgoing nurse did a handover and explained everything that had happened and the incoming nurse would say, 'Oh my god, that is a hell of a time you have been through.' The file on my trolley grew thick with notes.

I was really out of it most of the time — not sleeping and feeling weird. I loved having my family to visit. The day before I came home, friends came. One of them was Karen, my colleague with Tuesdays on Tedder, a weekly networking meeting we run. She brought beautiful gifts and flowers from everyone in the group. My other friend, Jan, brought food that was so much better than hospital food, along with sparkling water. My husband brought me flowers the first night. Unfortunately, I never got to see them again because I had been whisked to the operating room and spent the rest of the time in ICU. Luckily Molly had taken a photo of the lovely flowers given to me.

Hearing Others Struggling to Relearn

After my stay, I realised a lot of people who had had strokes also underwent carotid artery surgery. Many were quite a bit older than me. Some were learning how to walk again and having trouble speaking or comprehending language.

I found out my blocked carotid artery contained a web-like structure, which was cut out during the surgery. It had probably been there since birth. It was a congenital thing, more than a buildup of cholesterol. As I grew older the web-like structure was closing the artery off. The reason for the initial swelling was a facial vein that had been accidentally nicked during surgery. The other swellings occurred because of the way my body had latched onto the tube. It was just put down to one of those things that happen rarely, and I was just unlucky that it happened so many times. However, as my surgeon said, 'You were lucky that the GP had picked up the bruit in your neck.' That vascular sound is what had alerted him to send me for the tests in the first place. 'Someone up there was looking after you,' he said.

Divine Diversion

During my recovery, the hospital chaplain came to see me one day. I was surprised that she came to see me. After we chatted for a while, I asked why she came to see me. 'You have been through such an ordeal,' she said. 'The first surgery was major surgery, and then to have all the multiple times in the operating theatre within a week… It has been a very traumatic time for you.'

I realised that I had probably been better at handling the whole situation than I may have been a long time ago. I didn't know how much strength I had developed from other challenges that have happened over the years.

The chaplain had a lovely sense of calmness about her. We chatted about a retreat she was going on that weekend. It was actually a non-speaking retreat (little did I know I would have my own silent retreat later on in April). We chatted about mobile phones, computers, taking time off from these, helping people, leading a busy life and how important it is to 'unplug' sometimes and 'switch off.' It was a coincidence as a friend of mine had given me a crystal before I went into hospital to keep near the modem at home. It was shaped like a pyramid and absorbs electrical energy. The chaplain told me that as a coach and personal stylist who helped others, it was so important to take time for myself. I found her comforting. She didn't even look like a chaplain. I don't know what a chaplain supposed to look like, but she was very stylish and elegant.

She continued chatting about keeping life simple and appreciating the good things. This is what I believe, too. As a life coach, I believe that it's the people in your life who are important. After the events of that week, being in intensive care and having those multiple trips to the operating theatre, I realised how important the good people in my life are and how precious life is. I have always been more spiritual than religious. When I was a child, my family attended church on Sundays and my dad took us to the art gallery afterward. I went to confirmation classes and was baptised and confirmed. We didn't talk religion at home, but I have always had an open mind and known there is a higher power. I prayed to God during that last time in the operating theatre, and I feel thankful to have come through everything so far.

My Lucky Number

When Pete came to take me home on March 10, he brought Teddy with him. I couldn't help but notice the date: One week after I went in, and I emerged four surgeries later. Now, I was up to my tenth surgery. Ten is my lucky number. I felt lucky, that's for sure. I was so grateful to have come out of the ordeal and to know that I wasn't going to have any more surprises or to get wheeled into the operating theatre again. I was so pleased to see Pete and Teddy and had him on my lap the whole way home.

Pete also brought the *Femininessence* magazines, which featured me in an article. I was on the back cover of the March issue and had missed out on the launch event because I was in hospital for longer than expected. I asked the guy who wheeled me out to take a couple of copies up to the nurses in Ward 11. I was so relieved to get home to recover. The surgeon had told me to expect full recovery to take 9 to 12 months. As I am writing this, it is exactly one year to the week. My neck has healed up really well, and I used frankincense and helichrysum oils every day to reduce the scar.

At this point, all that had happened was Teddy had a broken leg and I had a week in the hospital where I'd nearly died and had had to have four surgeries. What I never saw coming was that a few weeks later, I would break my wrist. Somewhere in the midst of this, I needed to get my voice back.

April 2021 — Vipassana

While my wrist was still in a splint, I concentrated on trying to get my voice better. I gargled. I did voice exercises. I rested my voice as much as possible. The number of times that I had been intubated with the first surgeries had caused trauma to my vocal cords and my voice was getting worse and worse and it was becoming almost non-existent.

I regained my voice after some good advice and knowing people who knew all about vocal cords and the trauma that can happen to them.

Have you heard of an otolaryngologist? I hadn't. It is another name for an ear, nose and throat specialist.

One of my dear friends, Diane, has a daughter-in-law who is a speech pathologist. She offered to put us in touch. I had also spoken with another speech pathologist, Jenny Mathews, about how to minimise the damage to my vocal cords.

I found everything these speech experts said to be really helpful. I will always know now how to look after my vocal cords.

I was lucky enough to be able to get in to see a really good otolaryngologist in Brisbane. The surgeon I saw specialised in trauma to vocal cords.

When your voice becomes strained, it can cause damage. This is why singers, teachers or speakers can develop polyps on their vocal cords. At my appointment he sprayed aesthetic down my throat. It was the worst thing I have ever tasted. Then he put a tiny camera right down my throat and got to me make several sounds with my voice such as 'ahhhhhhhh' and 'eeeeeeeee.' It only lasted a couple of minutes, thank goodness. On the colour monitor, he showed me that what I had were granulomas due to trauma from the surgeries. They were so severe that they would be unlikely to go away naturally. We made the decision to book in for surgery on May 28. I had been asked to do an interview for a coach who was holding a women's summit, and

I had postponed it due to my voice being so bad. It was pretty much non-existent by that time. I explained to her I was going for surgery and was hoping to be okay after two weeks of complete voice rest. The surgery went well. I was able to do the interview after my two-week check-up. I actually did the interview that afternoon of my check-up. It was the first time I had spoken properly in weeks. I am absolutely thrilled to have my voice back and proud of myself for not talking at all for two weeks. I called it my own 'vipassana.' Voilà, I have my voice back! I feel so very blessed.

For a while, I had a plate in my left wrist from the break and Teddy had a plate in his right leg from his break. We had quite a start to the year. I did have the plate removed from my wrist as the hand surgeon who operated strongly recommended it. The plate was close to the tendon, and he didn't want that to rupture.

By the time I had minor surgery to remove the plate, I was more relaxed about going into theatre because the vocal cord surgery had been so successful.

I had had seven surgeries in three months. The first four happened in one week. 2021 was proving to be a year like no other, and that is what life is all about: You never know what each year is going to bring,

Five years earlier, I faced what I thought would be my toughest health challenge. At the time, I really didn't think anything could compare. That was the Tarlov cyst surgery. That is probably the origin of my resilience. It was like muscle training. The more you use it the stronger it gets. I believe resilience is like this. It all started with a park run...

5.
RESILIENCE AND CHOICES

Over the past few years, I have made some important choices. I am a firm believer that we all have choices. Whether those choices are right or wrong at the time is personal and each of us can only make certain choices for ourselves for whatever reason. It can take time to feel confident in yourself and know that you are making the right choice. It is only by actually making a choice that you think is the right one that you learn the consequences. Some of the most important choices we make are to do with our health. The reason I am sharing what follows is so that I can encourage you to take notice of your own body and keep researching until you discover what answers are available and right for you. This is what I feel has equipped me for whatever may happen in life. In 2015 for the first time, I experienced some serious health issues which came at a time when I was starting to discover new interests, start my new business and was enjoying being a grandmother to my first three grandchildren.

I had also started to enjoy going on five-kilometre Saturday morning runs held in various local parks. I also did a couple of charity run/walks.

After doing a few of these runs, I thought I had pulled a muscle or something as I started to get very acute and debilitating pain in the lumbar region of my back. It turned out to be a synovial cyst, which had lodged in my spine at L4-L5. I had massage, acupuncture and injections to try to get rid of the pain. Usually, these cysts do not cause a problem however as this one had lodged in the spine and the only option according to the surgeon I saw was to remove the cyst and fuse the spine. He said that to remove the cyst he would have to take some bone out and that would weaken that area of the spine. That was the reason for the spinal fusion. The pain was becoming more frequent, acute and debilitating. A friend recommended a surgeon who even doctors themselves go to for treatment. The surgery would be minimally invasive, with less cutting of the bone and muscle. Spine stability would not be affected, and spinal fusion would not be necessary. In February 2015, after much research, I went to the United States to undergo this surgery by the recommended surgeon. My recovery went well. I followed instructions and although it was major surgery, the incision was small and I was able to carry on with life as before. I was told to avoid high-impact exercises such as running. This was disappointing as I had been planning on getting more into running.

However, I was pleased to have had the surgery and did everything possible to maintain my health and keep fit. I thought this was the end of my spinal problems as we had been able to fix it the best way possible. I didn't have the acute pain anymore but the constant sciatica was still there. It was constant and severe. There was no let-up despite doing all the right exercises and eating healthily. I tried to forget about it and carry on with life but it got worse and worse no matter what I did. Sitting or standing for more than a few minutes at a time became unbearable. Every day, it was getting worse. I went back to my GP, who recommended another MRI which showed that I actually had Tarlov cysts in the sacrum area. The synovial cyst had been masking the underlying pain of the Tarlov cyst. The neurosurgeon that I went to see in Brisbane said this was definitely the cause of my pain. She said this had been there all the time but the first MRI report hadn't mentioned it. The first MRI only mentioned the synovial cysts, which were a separate issue, higher up and lodged in the bone part of the spine. These Tarlov cysts were in the nerves and in the sacrum area.

This neurosurgeon said no surgeon in Australia would operate as it was too risky and that I would need to be on strong painkillers for the rest of my life. She said that if I was someone who liked to keep busy and think a lot, if I were to take the strong painkillers I may 'even have trouble making a cup of tea.' Those were her words. I felt very upset and depressed about this. I was not happy with this as an answer and felt that this was not an option for me. I did not want to go under a pain management team as she had recommended or to take strong painkillers like that for the rest of my life.

Eventually, Tarlov cysts can eat away at the sacrum and you can end up in a wheelchair. I researched and found a Dr Frank Feigenbaum from Dallas, United States who only ever does Tarlov cyst surgery. I made contact with his office and had calls with his practice nurse who asked me to send the MRI via a system to deposit the images. Dr Feigenbaum wanted me to have a nerve block on the precise nerve affected to eliminate any likelihood of other issues causing the pain. The nerve block worked. This meant that there were no other reasons for the pain. Dr Feigenbaum operates on all international patients at a hospital facility in Cyprus called the American Institute for Minimally Invasive Surgery (AMIS). The reason is that it is more central to patients from Europe as well. By an amazing coincidence, two other ladies from Australia were suffering a similar condition. (It only affects 3 per cent of the population, mainly women). They were researching at the same time as me and ended up going to Cyprus for this life-changing surgery in the same week. One of them shared a room with me at the American Institute of Minimally Invasive Surgery (AMIS) She was in having her surgery when I arrived at the hospital in Cyprus. So, exactly 12 months after my first surgery in USA I found myself at the Brisbane airport heading to a different country for what I thought was the scariest time of my life. I really did think that was the biggest health crisis I would ever have.

When I went to Cyprus and Dr Feigenbaum operated, he found five Tarlov cysts in that area. 'If you have any in other areas, they will not cause an issue,' I was told. The spinal canal around the sacrum area is very small, and that is why it is a problem to have any cysts there.

Successful Result

The surgery on 3 February 2016 successfully halted the growth of the cysts. Many people suffer from diseases or conditions that are not commonly known. I had a wonderful GP who was not familiar with Tarlov cyst disease but was open to learning about it. She proved to be a great liaison with Feigenbaum's clinic in making sure we had the right pre- and post-op MRI and diagnostic protocols in place. I was grateful for this and she appreciated having all the information that I gave to her as she was so unfamiliar with the disease. I have now fully recovered from the surgery and initially had sciatica most days. Ensuring that I keep active and do Pilates regularly has helped tremendously.

Sea Change

Just before we moved to the coast, we used to make an hour-long trip early in the morning to drive down the coast, go for a swim in the ocean, have breakfast and go back to the city before we started our day. Years ago, when we were super busy with the business, we used to speak about what we'd like to do when we sold the family home, we often talked about moving to the coast. All the events that led up to where we live now meant that we moved there sooner rather than later. It has been the best decision as we are young enough to enjoy doing what we do.

When we made the decision to move, the real estate agent sold our house quickly even before it went to auction. We then started looking at apartments at the Gold Coast. There were some apartments, which were not big enough as we had been used to a very large house. We wanted to make sure that there was enough room for our daughters and their families for when they wanted to come and stay. The apartment we ended up buying was perfect. We have storage at a workshop we built nearby for a lot of the photos that we brought from the house. We have family photos and a lovely photo of my mother-in-law and my mum together from when I used to drive my mum over to visit my mother-in-law. We have a family photo of when the girls were young, the girl's graduation photos, all sorts of family memorabilia that we wanted to keep. My husband and I spent a long time deciding where to put the photos on the wall downstairs at our new place. We don't like calling it a place of work; it's really for our interests. Each of us has a business, which is also something that we really love to do. I've held weekend workshops and have a meeting room upstairs. I intend to hold more workshops there as well. It's a lovely space. And I feel very creative when I go to work there.

New Addition to the Family

Since everything that happened in 2021, with Teddy being such a playful guy and a special dog in our life, we felt he could do with a playmate. A coaching college friend of mine had asked about Teddy's breeders. We get a lot of questions about where we got him as he is such a good-natured dog. I phoned the breeder and enquired. I was told that Teddy's mum had just had a litter of puppies, and it was with the same Toy Poodle dad. After a day of thinking about it even more, we decided it would be wonderful to have a companion for Mr Ted. So, along with my friend picking up her puppy, I picked up little Miss Daisy. Teddy, my husband and our granddaughter Charlie came too. Teddy was great with Daisy straight away. It has turned out to be a great decision. Teddy and Daisy are best mates. She was the runt of the litter but very feisty and chases everywhere after Teddy which is what he loves. He has someone to do his favourite thing with: play chasing.

Now, Teddy sleeps at the foot of our bed and Daisy sleeps up near us on the pillow, We have to wake them up instead of the other way around. Teddy is trained to do many tricks, such as sitting, high-five and shake hands. My husband brushes the dogs every day. I don't know who enjoys that routine more – him or the dogs. We so enjoy them, as do our grandchildren and the rest of the family.

Oceans of Possibility

At our home on the Gold Coast, we have a gorgeous view of the ocean from the front windows, down the south coast from the southern balcony and a different view of the bridge and harbour from the northern balcony. I can look out the window, think of going for a walk on the beach and do just that in five minutes. There is a friendly village atmosphere, and it is a very relaxed lifestyle.

Every day, the ocean looks different. Sometimes, it is a deep cerulean blue with velvety gentle waves with white crests. Other days, it is grey, with thundery huge waves crashing into the sand. Sometimes like today as I write, I look out, and the ocean is a silvery sparkly blue, twinkling and inviting me to come down for a walk or a swim. Life is good and now, in my sixties, I can definitely say that the changes from day to day are fantastic.

It is amazing to think that having a dog never entered my realm of possibility. There were always other things that I wanted to do. Raising a family and having a successful business, living a life that was fulfilling and accomplished was important to me. Having good relationships and reaching goals were important to me. Travel was something I loved and still do. With current COVID travel restrictions, I am realising how lucky we were to have travelled to other places in the world. We have taken Teddy on a road trip and will take Daisy with us too, as they are both adaptable and enjoy being around us, whether we are at home or at work.

We have our fur babies, Teddy and Daisy, an apartment we love that has a fireplace to keep us cosy in the wintertime, hobbies and interests and the ability to have our family stay here. We know what it's like to lead a fulfilling life. It is busy, and we know to keep stress at bay, even during trying times.

Resilience and Choices

You learn about other countries by actually being there and meeting the local people and learning about their culture. However, adjusting to travelling less and spending more time at home, especially with our dogs, has opened up new possibilities. It has made me learn more about myself and the world I live in that may not be as broad physically but it is broader mentally and emotionally. I have slowed down and appreciate life as it is. When you slow down to become aware of all the possibilities that are right there around you, the world becomes a richer and even more exciting place.

Life is good. We enjoy exercising, going for walks and to the local markets or the dog beach or park on Sundays. Each day brings new and exciting possibilities because I appreciate every new day and what it may bring. I feel that I am ready for anything and am stronger and wiser than ever before. I am grateful for all the experiences and challenges. I am so grateful to Teddy, Daisy and all the friends, clients and wonderful people in my world of course starting with my husband and daughters and families. I feel very blessed to have six beautiful grandchildren, and I hope that this book will be a legacy for them.

My advice through these experiences is to advocate for your own health. Investigate, research and decide what is best for you personally. You only have one life, and it is your responsibility. Trust yourself implicitly to make the right decisions for *you*. Research well and then make an informed decision. No matter how qualified people may be, everything needs to make sense to you. Everyone has a choice and from those choices make your own decision. By all means, gather information and find out as much as you can, but consult with yourself as well as the professionals. You know your own body better than anyone when it comes to how you are feeling. All the decisions I have made so far regarding my health have been the right ones. I listen to my own body and take notice of what is going on for me. I intend to live the best life possible which living a balanced well-rounded and healthy life.

Other important lessons I have learned from experience and from my training are to be found in the following chapters. I want to share them with you so that you can understand that any challenge or problem in life can be overcome. In mathematics, all problems all have a solution. The solution may not be obvious straight away. It may be that with the right mindset you will find that something completely different works out much better than what you thought it might. It all comes down to having a sense of curiosity and a lot of courage and belief in yourself and your ability to cope with challenges and changes.

Part 2

6.
THE STRATEGY

Changing Events

There have been episodes in my life where I have learned lessons and become wiser and more compassionate towards myself and others. In doing so, I am generating my own personal power.

Celebrating the Negative Events in Life

If events have had an emotional impact, people are more likely to remember them. If that memory can then be stored in a positive way instead of negative this serves a purpose, instead of becoming a memory that will weigh you down. Create a pattern of being a creator, not a victim, in your life. This is a strategy that definitely does work. Celebrate the emotional events. You can keep the truth of a story in your life and celebrate the positives to alter what could have otherwise been a negative memory.

Share Your Experience to Help Yourself and Others

I received useful information by letting others know what was happening in my life. Instead of hiding my rapidly deteriorating vocal cords, I let it be known and then was told about someone who could help me. I can now share the experience in the hope that it may help others. I shared the experience of getting treatment for Tarlov cyst disease in an article. Someone read about it and contacted me. He wanted help for his wife who was in debilitating pain from the same disease. He was able to ask me questions, and I put him in touch with others who had the same treatment and also the support group. I gave him information about my experience. He asked other people and then accessed professional advice. He and his wife were then able to make a more informed decision about treatment and she also had treatment with the same doctor.

Ways to Rewrite the Story

Events that happen in your life can be accounted for with a result that serves us no matter how negative those events are. By including Teddy in my account of the trying times from February through to April, it took away the intensity from the health issues I encountered. I learned to include something positive which was the fact that Teddy leaving the puddle of wee put a comical spin on something that could otherwise have been a heavy scary and dramatic memory for me. Teddy is so precious to me and me feeling so bad about his accident took the trepidation away that I had about my surgery. I choose to see everything that happened then and prior to that year as the development of resilience. Teddy brought everything into perspective. Slipping on that puddle and having to have another surgery straight after that week from hell with the other ones helped me get over my fear of operating theatres. Then I had the successful vocal cord surgery and removal of the plate. Done and dusted! There are many ways to rewrite the story and it takes some rising above how you feel at the time to see that there is a lighter side to life even when everything seems dark and heavy. Colour the events with lightness instead.

What Not to Do

When certain events happened in my younger years, I thought I could make the memories go away by pretending they happened to someone else. All this did was suppress the awful memory only for it to crop up later on when I had daughters who reached the same age as I was back then. The subconscious mind suppresses memories or 'pretends' things didn't happen to keep us safe. As soon as it thinks enough time has passed, that memory will bubble up from a trigger. The trigger could be something that you would think may be completely unrelated to the event. It could even be a smell, a vision or someone saying something. It could be when you are watching a movie or a show. It could be hearing of an event similar to what happened and you immediately relate it to your life. If you push those triggered memories away all the time it can cause all sorts of issues including emotional, mental and physical issues.

Two Types of Lying

By pretending events didn't happen or by suppressing them, you are actually lying to yourself. There are two ways to lie: by commission or omission. Commission is actually telling a lie, and omission is leaving something out completely. This leads to distrusting what your mind is telling you. Acknowledge what happened and accept any feelings that crop up. Name those emotions. Studies have shown that naming your emotion immediately changes the stress involved. It gives you more clarity and makes the emotion less intense. You can think and feel in a more effective way that serves you positively rather than stifling your ability to move forward. Unresolved feelings of fear, anxiety, anger, sadness and guilt can stop you from progressing in life. If you name what you are feeling, look at whether the reason for that emotion still exists or whether it is something your brain perceives as a threat because of what you experienced in the past. This way, you can face up to the events and see the past for what it is without having fear of the emotions it brings up. Honesty is always best especially when it comes to being honest with yourself. Constantly keeping this in mind ensures that you are always facing reality and dealing with what *is*. You can become consistently stronger in your ability to face facts, therefore trusting in yourself even more. The most important person to trust is yourself and that is what gives you confidence in life and the ability to trust other people.

Benefits of Change

If you have experienced a huge change in your life, find a way to be excited by possibilities and the new ways you can adapt. COVID-19 affected many small and large businesses. People's lives were changed and ways of doing business altered so much. 'Pivot' became a new buzzword during and following the pandemic. This means that many companies turned their business around by providing more online services and catering to the needs of their customers and clients in a different way. This either served them in the short term or ensured long-term resilience and growth of the business.

Restaurants changed to takeaway, deliveries and catering. This meant a change in the number and type of staff. When the rules during the pandemic changed to restaurants being open again after lockdowns, owners were finding that they had staff shortages instead of excess staff. The same with retail stores. During the pandemic, many stores offered more online shopping and lockdowns forced customers to shop online.

When the doors were open again, shoppers looked forward to shopping and retailers had to adjust their stock levels to cope with demand. Many gyms, yoga and Pilates studios offered online classes. Ours did during the lockdown, and now some are still livestreaming classes, which has benefited many people who live in remote areas. This became an extra service.

The companies that were able to adapt, change their ways of doing things — in other words, 'pivot' — were able to better cater for remote working, social distancing and more prevalent use of technology.

Flexibility

Being flexible and adaptable is something that I have found to be a useful personality trait. By learning about yourself and knowing your boundaries, you can afford to be flexible and still keep your boundaries. Adapting to situations will hold you in good stead in life.

The Only Constant Is Change

We live in a world that is constantly changing, and if we try to fight that change, we will only end up frustrated and depressed. How can we possibly know for certain everything that is going to happen? That is impossible. Change can create new beginnings.

> *'Change is the only constant in life.'*
> **– Heraclitus, Greek philosopher**

Accepting What Is

Accepting a current situation is part of creating a feeling of peace within. I was told something by a psychologist which resonated with me. 'Expecting something to be different to what is and not accepting the facts is a version of hell,' he said. This is so true. Instead of fighting against what is, we can look at things with a different perspective.

Realising that Nothing Is Permanent

As well as being flexible and adaptable, I realised that impermanence is a part of life. Become an expert at finding the gift in change and new beginnings. After all, nothing, absolutely nothing, is ever permanent. Nothing remains exactly the same as it always was.

The Choices We Make

Life is full of twists and turns. It is how we cope with those twists and turns, the choices we make every second of every day, that creates the life we live. It is the 'right now' that is important and growing wiser with each new experience.

Training for More of Life

The events that happen in your life prepare you for more of life. It is like constant training. The key is to have the right mindset as you are dealing with the curve balls that life throws at you. Strength and resilience don't happen overnight. Being self-aware and having a sense of curiosity is where it starts. We must also realise that we are human 'becomings' as well as human beings. Just 'being' and existing each day is not enough. Taking an interest in yourself, in your interactions with others and human behaviour makes everyone more understanding and much wiser. Wanting to always understand more about how we feel is good training too because our brains release dopamine and other feel-good chemicals when we encounter new things. Being curious and aware helps us to deal with a constantly changing world. This is the way to achieve more resilience and happiness.

The Best Pieces of a Broken World

In October 2021, I had an opportunity to give an online TEDx talk titled *The Best Pieces of a Broken World*. Something I felt passionate about was how life has changed during COVID. I spoke about the economic insecurity, disruption to every aspect of life and the challenges to mental and physical health people were experiencing. By focusing on simple concepts from different cultures, many people over the years have been able to cope with change and enhance life for the better to repair and heal.

When times are tough, think of the best pieces of your world and focus on them. By being grateful for and appreciating what you already have, you will attract more of that into your life.

Laughter is the Best Medicine

From my own experience, turning the events that happened bang, bang, bang, one after the other in quick succession into something humorous has lightened up life. This is a choice that I have made. To look back at this time and smile. *Teddy's Revenge* is my way of changing the story by naming it. The simple narrative put all the events that happened within those short months in a completely different light for that period of the year. Although it meant the rest of the year was not what I had planned it to be it was beneficial because I learned a valuable lesson to look at the funny side of what happened. I can now use a metaphor to ensure I make something positive out of something that could have easily had a negative impact.

Making Light Out of Dark Subjects

Calamities happen, and it would be impossible to see many of them as funny or 'cute' such as I did with *Teddy's Revenge*. I understand this and do not wish to play down how serious many events in life are. When possible If we can see some things from the funny side, it makes them less threatening in our minds. My husband and I recently watched a British comedy series, *After Life*, written and produced by comedian Ricky Gervais. The topics involved death, grief, loss and depression. The characters became familiar as it was set in a small village in England. The key message from the series was that life goes on. It was a comedy yet it dealt with subjects that are usually such a serious part of life.

Our daughter told us about *Derek,* also directed by and starring Ricky Gervais. Most of the actors were the same as the actors in *After Life*. Again, viewers get very attached to the characters in the series, which depicts residents and workers in a retirement home. It was a mockumentary and comedy about people who are marginalised and excluded from mainstream society. The main character, Derek, is kind and socially awkward. He completely lacks inhibition and is someone to whom you warm to. The series deals with aging, death, loneliness and mental health issues, but because it's a comedy, it deals with all these topics in a light, heart-warming way.

Reframing

Looking at the funny side of things is simply a way to 'reframe' a situation. Neuro-linguistic progamming (NLP) coaches use the term 'reframe' to metaphorically put something into a different frame. If you imagine something in an ugly frame or a frame that doesn't fit with the way you want to see things. You can take that situation and reframe it into something far more attractive, something that serves you and that you can use to make your life even better. Reframing gives us the opportunity to be quite creative by imagining how we can possibly put a situation in a positive light or find the positive intention in a situation that might otherwise seem negative. For example, instead of saying, 'I am stuck at home and can't go out anywhere because my car has broken down,' you can reframe it to, 'I am getting my car fixed so this gives me an opportunity to get some things done around the house.'

Diffusing the Situation

We can choose to reframe either through humour or by disassociating and seeing the situation from another perspective. This separates our emotion from the event and enables us to see it in a different context. This is what I did with the parade of events that happened in 2021: Teddy's broken leg, surgery that went wrong, three more surgeries in one week, damaged vocal cords, slipping and breaking wrist, repairing the break and vocal cord surgery after that. I chose to think of that time as 'Teddy's Revenge' which has helped me to look at things from a different perspective.

Those Energising Endorphins

I have some wonderful friends with whom I can laugh and have great conversations. Being able to laugh at life and aspects of it is a skill that can make life so much easier. Laughing until your belly hurts and you have tears coming down your face is a feeling that everyone can experience. Can you identify with this? Have you had a time when something has happened or you have watched something funny and laughed like this? How did you feel afterward? Your endorphins probably increased. You may be with a friend when this happens, and it is difficult to even talk, you are both laughing so much. This provides a total distraction from the tougher, more serious side of life. I believe this is what has kept my mum, who is in her mid-nineties, so young at heart. She has a great sense of humour.

If you watch one of the YouTube compilations of 'contagious laughter', you will see what I mean. My favourites are the videos of a baby laughing at paper ripping. You can even google that one. I remember trying this when I was minding my eldest grandson when he was in a bouncinette. I knelt down in front of him and started ripping paper. He absolutely had that same belly laugh, which in turn made me laugh, then he laughed even more. I showed my daughter when she came to pick him up. We were all in fits of laughter and it felt so good. I actually think the sound of babies or children laughing is one of the best sounds in the world.

This is a reason why having dogs is so beneficial. They are always doing funny things and have such great characters. As well as the cuddles and patting of dogs they have such strong personalities that you cannot but smile when with them. My husband and I love playing with the dogs and enjoy their spontaneous energy.

> *'We do not stop playing because we grow old, we grow old because we stop playing.'*
>
> **– Benjamin Franklin**

Dr Lee Berk, associate professor at Loma Linda University in California, has spent nearly three decades studying the ways the aftershocks of a good laugh ripple through the brain and body.

Berk says your mind, endocrine (hormone) system and immune system are constantly communicating with one another in ways that impact everything from your mood to your ability to fend off sickness and disease. 'Laughter appears to cause all the reciprocal, or opposite, effects of stress,' Berk explains. He says laughter shuts down the release of stress hormones like cortisol. It also triggers the production of feel-good neurochemicals like dopamine, which have all kinds of calming, anti-anxiety benefits.

Many things can trigger laughter. Dr Robert Provine, a neuroscientist at the University of Maryland, Baltimore County, says you are 'thirty times more likely to laugh around other people than when you are by yourself.' This is probably also because the social connection of being with other people is another feel-good factor.

Social Connection

I have made a lot of new friends through the dogs. It is funny that in the area we live you, get to know the dogs' names before their owners'. One day, I was out taking Teddy for a walk and he met two other dogs about the same size. The owners and I started talking while Teddy played with the dogs called Huxley and Miley at the footpath. The lovely ladies invited me to have coffee with them. We caught up with another of their friends. I have since been to the movies, breakfast, lunches, dinner with these women and sometimes with our partners. All because the dogs got talking to each other — well, sniffing each other. Dogs are a real ice-breaker as you just start by asking the names of the dogs and their age and breed. When we were walking down to the café, a guy was walking behind us and commented, 'You ladies should have dogs with pink fur.' We realised then that we were all wearing pink T-shirts and jeans, and even the friend we met was wearing pink.

It was really funny. I guess it is like when your children start school a lot of friends are made with other parents through the children.

Moments of Connection

Having Teddy to look after, play with and train has given my husband and I another opportunity to connect even more with each other because we have a common love of him and now also his sister Daisy. On Sunday mornings, we love to take them to the dog beach, bath them and spend time looking after their grooming. Barbara Fredrickson talks about 'micro-moments of connection' in her Ted Talk, *Remaking Love*. No matter what you are doing together even if it is something as simple as cleaning up a mess, designing a room or cooking a meal those simple moments create intimacy and strengthen the love or bond between individuals. Its all about being open and having a common activity that you share together. Teddy and Daisy have given us the unexpected opportunity to connect in a completely different way even though we have been together for over 45 years.

7.
LIFE LESSONS

Each Year Is Different and That Is Life

As the years roll by, each one different from the last, it shows that we are living as we are meant to by really experiencing life. The year leading up to writing this book is proof that just because you have successfully come through challenges in your life that others will not happen. We are constantly being tested. Just like when you study at school or college the test or exam is so that you can use the information the study and learning has given you. The lesson isn't just so that you can pass or get through the test or the exam – it is to equip you with that skill afterwards, to apply it to future scenarios. Life will always be giving us tests and that is why we are constantly learning.

Have Gratitude for Challenges

Slipping on the tiles and having a broken wrist helped me get over my fear of the operating theatre. I was so grateful to be rid of the pain. That seems like a strange thing to say however it was one of the ways I choose to think about that incident. Thinking about it this way helps to ease the frustration of not being able to get done what I wanted to get done during that six-week period as well as recovering from the first time in hospital.

Communication Is Key

The right sort of communication makes all the difference in personal relationships, business relationships and life in general. I believe it is number one and clear honest communication means that any issue or challenge can be overcome. I have appreciated any time someone has communicated honestly with me and this has promoted a sense of trust. If anyone is dishonest and lacks integrity I have become more aware through that experience. The example of the surgeon being honest with me about how he felt is exactly what I mean. I had a huge amount of trust, even though I was afraid.

Work Out What Is Important

Each year seems to fly by faster and faster as we get older. It is a matter of using your time for what is important to you. We are born alone and we die alone, so make yourself a priority. This is not selfish. This is smart living. That way, we have the health and energy to help others – mentally, emotionally and physically. I have discovered that the cause of a lot of anxiety is thinking about what you 'should' be doing because of what others may think of you. Stop 'shoulding all over yourself' and just be you. I realised that I want to live life my way and am so grateful to have my life. I feel grateful to be me and to know that looking after myself enables me to better look after others. I have learned to listen to my gut and to say 'no' when I can feel that something doesn't serve me.

Do What You Love and Love What You Do

Work out what it is that you love doing and do it. There are times when we are in the process of discovering what we love and that is great as it is all part of the journey. If you don't love it anymore, use the experience and 'tweak' your life somehow to ensure it flows for *you*. I have been a team leader for a multi-level marketing (MLM) company. I still love the products and believe that MLM companies are good, despite some of the unfairly negative publicity they have received. It just wasn't right for me anymore and my heart wasn't in it. I found that I was only going for the incentive trip rewards and the goals set by the company to set a good example for my team. I could have spent years and years doing this, but I would have been living my life for others instead of for myself.

Be Open and Flexible

We teach best what we most need to learn. Be open to learning more each day. I am learning more and more from experiences. No one is perfect, and as Tony Robbins says, 'Constant and never-ending improvement,' is the answer to cultivating a growth mindset. As I wrote in my chapter that appeared in *How Becoming a Coach Changed My Life* by Glen Murdoch, we are all perfectly imperfect. That is the title of my chapter in that book. I used to think that being a life coach meant that I would have to be this perfect person who knew absolutely everything there was to know about life. That is impossible. For starters, no one is perfect, and we can never possibly know absolutely everything. We can, however, have fun learning. We can become richer inside by learning from the experiences and we gain subconscious learning from what we do day by day simply by living life to the fullest.

Do Not Judge Others

It is by judging other people that we are actually being judgemental ourselves and putting each person (and ourselves) in a box. Everyone is different and that is what makes the world such an interesting place. Be understanding of others. Have empathy while also maintaining your boundaries.

Be Kind

Be kind to everyone, as most people are fighting some kind of battle. We all have responsibilities, and the greatest responsibility is to ourselves and how we are able to respond to others and to situations. It is when we turn external influences back onto ourselves and blame ourselves that we are taking on stuff that doesn't belong to us. Being kind to yourself is as important as being kind to others.

Treat the Child with Care

> *'Caring for your inner child has a powerful and surprisingly quick result: Do it and the child heals.'*
> — **Martha Beck**

We all have an inner child who benefits from being looked after. This refers to the fact that our minds and bodies carry the memories, feelings and patterns from the past. The more you can know, understand and connect with yourself and the child within the healthier and happier you will be. Even if you don't refer to this as inner child work, you will know what it feels like when you practice self-care. According to the Cambridge Dictionary, 'Your kid within is the part of your personality that still reacts and feels like a child.'

Take Care of Your Own Business

Arguments or disagreements between other people are between others and do not involve you. Be supportive. Use discretion. Have your own opinions. I am very conscious of not getting involved in other people's arguments as there is usually their story and the other person's story and then there is the universe's story. If you try to look after what is not your business, then who is looking after your business?

Keep Friends in the Know

You don't know where support or the answer to a challenge is going to come from. If you keep everything to yourself and try to struggle on you may miss out on valuable information or recommendations someone could help you with. This was particularly evident when I was struggling with my voice and getting some help with this. It wouldn't have been repaired by itself. It was from letting people know that I was working out what to do that I found a great specialist.

Persevere and Patience

Healing and recovery can take time, so patience and doing the right thing definitely pays off. Being strict with myself by not talking for two weeks paid off in repairing my vocal cords. I was over the moon at being able to talk again with a full recovery.

Be patient with yourself when you are healing, and be patient with others also.

Deal with Each Situation as it Arises

Handling each incident as an individual event rather than lumping everything in together is the best way to handle challenges in life. It is like handling one day at a time, which stops you from being overwhelmed with the obstacles in your way. It really does help if you can expect the unexpected. Years ago, I used to lump everything into a huge pile that seemed unsurmountable. This was a long time ago, and it was something that only made matters worse. Through coaching and experience, I have learned what to do and what not to do. Creating that huge pile of everything you can think of is definitely not serving you and your life.

Expecting a 'Next' in Life

I remember a friend finding out she would have to move her family out of a house they were renting, and it was an extremely busy time in her life. The owner was selling the house and this friend would have to disrupt her business, which was based at home, and move fairly quickly. She sighed and looked at me, smiled when she was telling me about all the things that were happening and said, 'Sometimes, I roll with the punches and kind of expect unexpected things to happen and just say to myself… next!' I felt that this is a good way to think about life. It will not be smooth at any time, and if it is too smooth, what are we learning and what are we achieving? Look back on changes in life and reflect on how you coped with those changes, whether they were expected or a complete surprise, whether negative or positive.

8.
LOOK BACKWARD TO SEE FORWARD

'The farther back you can look, the farther forward you are likely to see.'

— **Winston Churchill**

Learning from experience is so valuable. Whatever happens, it is our reaction to the event, not the actual event, that has a lifelong effect. Learning the lesson does not mean that we need to keep thinking of the past. The past does not exist anymore. I like the analogy of a stream flowing past a point on a riverbank. Once the water in the stream passes that point it is not going back — it has gone. You can look back at the past and learn as long as you look forward as well and actually see forward. There is a difference between 'looking' and 'seeing.' The Oxford Dictionary's basic definition of 'looking' is to direct one's gaze in a specified direction. The definition of 'seeing' is the action of seeing someone or something. ... It has more to do with mental perception. Seeing is about noticing and looking is more of a direction.

Age of Influence

Many of our behaviours, habits and even most of our opinions are learned when we are young. From birth until seven years old we are influenced solely by our parents and environment. Other factors start to influence us from ages 7 to 14 and up. Our peers, friends, acquaintances, teachers, people we spend time with and experiences we go through shape and influence us during these formative years. Because of this, many of our beliefs that our subconscious minds accept as true are really not true. Those beliefs can be incomplete and flawed. It is these beliefs that operate our behaviours without us being consciously aware of it. I am a different person now to who I was 10, 20 or 30 years ago. Apart from the 'experience lines' on my face and the obvious physical changes you get from being older I am much wiser and more understanding than I ever was. I grew up with beliefs that didn't serve me, and I know that I put my parents through a tough time without considering what they were going through. My parents divorced when I was in my teens, which cannot have been an easy time for them. I spent a lot of time with my friends and had other influences that were not the best as I grew up. Looking back on that time has given me reason to explore the changes that people go through and how they develop as the years go by. I truly believe that we keep getting wiser as we get older as long as we keep taking notice and really seeing things instead of just looking and making judgment based on our past influences.

Make the Most of Challenges

The key to progressing in a positive way is to be able to get up, dust ourselves off or 'wash off the wee' and move on with life. I know that looking back at the past and dwelling there in your mind can cause depression, just as worrying about the future is a major cause of anxiety. Worrying is thinking about things that may never happen. Learn from the past and develop a healthy sense of detachment. I truly believe that a combination of my life experiences and my learnings as a trained life coach have given me the ability to be more pragmatic about events. We are all emotional beings and learning about emotional intelligence is something that cannot be read about in a book or learned in a classroom. Emotional intelligence comes from living life and experiencing emotions while being self-aware and taking notice of those emotions.

Embody the Lessons

Learning alongside living is the only true way to embody the lessons of life. Once those lessons are embodied and appreciated for what they are as lessons not to be forgotten that is what leads to a wiser and more emotionally intelligent life. I remember many aspects of coaching that have meant a lot to me. Many of you may be aware of the 'victim triangle' or 'drama triangle.' There is something very powerful that you can do, which is reframing that triangle and instead of being a victim of life, you can be a creator in your own life. Apply the rules of pure logic, which is the science of pure reason by using language to change an event or events to positive occurrences rather than negative and you can 'create' a valuable experience. You have the power to accept or reject the limits that you may have put on yourself as a result of your previous influences and beliefs. It is important to have self-awareness and understanding on a conscious level that the beliefs you have may very well be from external influences instead of your own.

Creating the Space

In his book, *Man's Search for Meaning*, Viktor Frankl stated that between 'stimulus and response there is a space. In that space is our power to choose our response. In our response lies our growth and our freedom.' An issue or problem develops when within that space you either accept or make up an accurate conclusion about yourself and buy into that belief that it must be true. After hearing about and reading *The Work* by Byron Katie, I now ask myself, 'Do I know this is true? Is it really, true? How do I know that it is really really true?' It is when we believe that there are no other possibilities apart from our belief that we are limiting ourselves. These unexamined beliefs stem from programmed responses from our childhood. Creating a space in between the event and the response gives us time to exercise an option or to use our personal power to re-evaluate our beliefs from the perspective of experience. Choosing to look at all the events that have happened in my life to date as opportunities to explore more possibilities will serve as a positive for my life rather than a negative. You can consciously choose to be optimistic about your circumstances. You can open your mind and allow yourself to see the goodness in all situations no matter how something turns out. Being self-aware is the starting point to work from. Self-awareness comes from a sense of curiosity.

Open Your Mind and Listen to What Your Body is Saying

Open your mind to be willing to consider all aspects of a situation, including how your body feels and what your head, heart and gut are telling you. In doing so, you will become more self-aware. If you keep yourself numb and 'safe' by not acknowledging your feelings, you are denying yourself the chance to explore and learn.

9.
TEDDY'S TIPS

These tips come from observing and living with Teddy and his way of life each day.

I recall going through a particularly difficult and lonely time in my life. I was driving down a main street around Christmas on a warm, still evening, almost midnight. I drove past a small church with lights all around it. The church looked so pretty, lit up with a sign of coloured lights that spelled out '*HOPE.*' For some reason, that always stuck in my mind, and ever since then I have liked the word hope.

Teddy's motivation is the hope of getting his favourite rewards of play, praise and tiny treats. Dog trainers say to give lots of praise when they do something right. Teddy likes to please, so he always sits on command because there is that hope of a reward. I taught him how to do a high-five and he learned it so well that every time you ask him to sit, he does the high-five and lifts his paw straight away.

There is always the hope of praise and a treat and that we will play tug of war with him or throw his favourite Bunny or Chicken. When we open the ice drawer in the freezer, he comes running because there is the hope of getting a piece of ice to crunch on. If he hears the word 'park,' 'walk,' 'car,' or 'beach,' he jerks his head up and his eyes brighten with the hope of immediately going there. If we don't leave straight away, he soon reminds us. So much of life is based on hope.

Hope as a Motivator

Advertisements and marketing use hope to sell products, promoting the sense that there is always something good on the horizon just waiting for you. Hope does require action to accompany it if you want something good. It is encouragement and positivity. Hope is uplifting. It creates a sense of energy and keeps us looking forward and not back. Optimism and hope are useful traits to have and the more you can focus on being optimistic and hopeful, the easier it will be to deal with any challenges that come your way. Some people believe that it is better to be pessimistic so that you are not disappointed when things don't turn as you hoped. Being overly optimistic may also give you a slightly distorted view of reality. I would much rather develop my optimism muscle than have a pessimistic view of life just to 'be on the safe side'. Holding hope in your heart creates that optimistic feeling no matter what is happening.

Teddy's Tip No. 1: 'Good things happen to those who do the right thing.'

Constant Curiosity

Dogs are constantly intrigued by the world around them. Every day, there are new and exciting things to look at do and smell. Mindfulness is so good for us. It is calming to notice surroundings, to notice flowers and lovely smells in a garden. Dogs are experts at mindfulness. They notice smells, sounds and every little thing that is going on. Notice how you are breathing slower when you are being present and noticing your surroundings. Notice how much more exciting life is when we become curious about how we can make a difference in our life and in the life of others. We can learn a lot from dogs by being curious about our own world.

Teddy's Tip No. 2: 'Smell everything, look at everything, listen to everything, touch and taste everything.'

Discernment

This is something that dogs are good with. I find that even friendly dogs can tell if someone loves dogs or doesn't. Dogs, as with most animals, are very intuitive. They love to run and play with each other but can sense if another dog or a person is not friendly or to be trusted. Appreciate what you have and value who you have in your world. If others are no longer in your life, there may be a good reason.

Teddy's Tip No. 3: 'If someone doesn't treat you right, keep away from them and especially don't sniff their bottom.'

A Dog With a Bone

One of the secrets to developing strength and resilience is to keep going with something that you are passionate about. If you know *why* you are doing what you're doing, this keeps you going when times are tough. When you absolutely know and trust the people in your world who love you and who you love back, you know what is precious to you. Be like Teddy when he wants something. He just goes for it and doesn't stop or run out of energy until he gets whatever he is chasing – usually Bunny or Chicken. That is by far the most important thing in the world to have that strength and resilience, to have the passion for your why and realise the power that you have inside of yourself. No one can take that power away from you.

Teddy's Tip No. 4: 'Go for it – Don't let anything stop you and eventually you'll get your prize.'

Focus on What You Want

That thing that you want to get is something that requires focus and determination. Teddy has this intent stare on Bunny or Chicken when it is about to be thrown – sometimes he catches it in mid-air. If you look at any dog watching something that is about to be thrown for them to go after their stare is unwavering. They are not distracted by other objects or sounds. They are determined with laser beam focus.

Teddy's Tip No. 5: 'One shiny bright object at a time.'

Routine Is Good

As a person who likes variety and spontaneity, I have come to appreciate how valuable and comforting having a routine can be. Dogs thrive on routine, and Teddy has a certain routine when it comes to getting brushed in the morning, waiting for Pete to throw him a pair of socks so that he can run with them out to the kitchen, which is where Pete puts his socks and shoes on.

Teddy's Tip No. 6: 'Its fun to know what happens at what time because then I can be ready for it.'

Building Rapport

Just like humans, dogs seem to match and mirror each other. Teddy and his sister, Daisy, like to lie in almost exactly the same positions, sometimes not far from each other. They will stare at you the same way and seem to be able to sense where you are and what you are doing so that they can join in. As humans, it is easier to build rapport if we can be flexible and fit in with another person's way of doing things sometimes. It is interesting to watch how dogs do this with one another.

Teddy's Tip No. 7: 'Life is more fun when you spend time and play with others.'

Moving On

Dogs don't hold grudges. They are like children in that they react and then move on. Just like children and adults they do remember. If they have been poorly treated, they will remain wary of similar people or things in future. This is different from holding a grudge. The only time I have seen Teddy holding a grudge was when we took him on a long road trip. He slept between us in the car and was with both of us 24/7 for ten days. He was fussed over everywhere we went and loved going with us. When we arrived home, I went out and got some shopping and Pete went to wash the car in the workshop. Teddy went and sat in his canvas crate and wouldn't come out for quite a while. He really was grumpy that we weren't on holiday anymore.

Teddy's Tip No. 8: 'You can be grumpy and then happy all in five minutes. It's easy if you have people to love, so take each day as It comes.'

Keeping Life Simple

According to the American Veterinary Medical Association, the first year of a medium-sized dog's life is equal to about 15 years of a human's life. The second year of a dog's life is equivalent to about nine human years. After that, every human year equals approximately four or five dog years. They seem to make the most out of every day and appreciate companionship, food, water, shelter and a comfortable place to sleep. They love playing and finding joy every day, which is so lovely to be around. Dogs know how to play and have fun. It is natural for them to exercise when they have energy and to rest when they need it.

Teddy's Tip No. 9: 'Run, run, run until you are tired, then stop and rest – easy as that.'

Worrying is a Waste of Time

When thinking of getting a dog, we went through all the pros and cons. One of the cons of being a dog owner is that we thought we wouldn't be able to leave him at home if we had to go out. Once Teddy was past the young puppy stage, he was great when we went out because he was used to it. I would purposely go out for five or ten minutes to start with and then come back in so that he knew that all was going to be okay. If we had always made sure there was someone there, he would not be used to the change of us not being there and would fret and worry. Instead of worrying about the future, accept that there will always be uncertainty. Just like Teddy not knowing when we would be back, he knew that we would come back. Instead of worrying about what might happen and the 'what ifs' in life, we can think, 'No matter what, things will be okay.' A dog has no control over what time we will go out and when we will be back. He has no control over what happens, he remains happy and content. We have no control over what happens and if we can relax and remain content in this knowledge, life is much easier to handle.

Teddy's Tip No. 10: 'If you don't like something, let people know – Things may change and if they don't, find a way to adapt.'

10.
LIFE TOOLS AND GIFTS

The Gift of Experience

If you experience a series of negative events that happen one after the other in your life, it can be too easy to expect that this is just the way it is. It isn't. You can turn negative events into something extremely valuable. A lesson learned through experience is a gift. You can create something to always serve you positively from past experiences. You can use the lessons to develop a strength that you never knew you had. No amount of reading or attending courses, listening to podcasts or watching YouTube videos can replace actually physically, emotionally and mentally going through something yourself. You develop an awareness about circumstances and empathy with other people who may be experiencing something similar.

Be an Observer

Looking at your life with a sense of 'observing', rather than internalising and making meaning of events that happen is going to work better for you. Develop tools to counteract and break the cycle.

See the World Like an Artist

Artists talk about perception: the way we look at a situation or an event. One artist will look at a scene and paint it in a completely different way to another artist. The Merriam-Webster thesaurus defines perception as follows: 'Perception not only creates our experience of the world around us; it allows us to act within our environment. Perception is very important in understanding human behaviour because every person perceives the world and approaches life problems differently. 'By standing back and observing a situation, we are able to develop a better perception. This is much easier than being right 'in' a situation. This way we can see a situation or event from different viewpoints. You will find a powerful exercise to practise this under the next heading.

Triangle of Wisdom Exercise

Arrange three chairs in a triangle. Choose one chair to be the first position (this is you), another to be second position (this is your fear or worry about something) and the final chair in the third position (the impartial observer). This is called perceptional positioning. Once sitting in the first position, you tell the second position (chair) why you don't want the fear or worry. Then go and sit in the second position and imagine you are the fear or worry and that you have a positive intention for the first position. There is a good reason for why you are trying to frighten or worry the first position. Be curious about what it could be as you sit in the second chair position. Next, return to the first position and respond to this. You can switch chairs a few times until you really understand the positive intention and have felt, explored, understood and responded to it. When you have finished, go and sit in the third position and comment as the impartial observer on what you have observed. How would you suggest, as the impartial observer, that the first position person could find a way to meet the positive intention without the fear?

You can try this yourself the next time you want to get a different perspective on something.

Despite the challenges you may face in your life, the biggest and most complex obstacle you will ever have to personally overcome is your own mind. You aren't responsible for everything that happens to you in life, but you *are* responsible for how you handle those challenges. There are ways to change how you think and feel.

How we think affects our emotions, and our emotions affect our behaviour. This is called the neurolinguistic programming cybernetic loop. The mind/brain and body interact and affect each other. They are not distinct, and what affects one affects the other. You cannot change one of these things without changing the others.

You can break the cycle of negative feelings (internal state) by adjusting your thought patterns (internal processing) by using physiology (external behaviour). This includes something as simple as adjusting your posture. In her TED talk, Amy Cuddy talks about the 'power pose,' which involves stretching out and up to make yourself feel more powerful and dominant. Cuddy relates to the animal kingdom in her talk. Dogs tend to make themselves bigger (even small dogs do this), walk faster and hold their head up when they see something they want to bark at. Cuddy advises using the power pose of stretching up, holding the head up and placing hands on the hips for two minutes before doing something like going for a job interview or going onstage.

Once I moved from intensive care and eventually left the hospital, I felt so much better as I was able to move around. I was able to resume some of my normal activities and this felt so good.

Movement is so important as it affects how we think and feel. Positive body language, movement and our physiology go hand-in-hand with psychology and positive emotions.

The Gift of a Simple Smile

When you are feeling depressed or sad, it can show on your face. If you are feeling happy or excited, you glow and your eyes shine. Something as simple as smiling can change the way you feel and think, and how others respond to you. I have noticed that people smile at Teddy when we take him for a walk. Teddy smiles when he has been to the park or the beach. He might be exhausted but he has his mouth open, his tongue hanging out, his eyes wide and it shows on his face how happy he is. I enjoy the fact that other people get pleasure from seeing happy dogs. People always ask me if they can pat Teddy. It makes me smile to see him first thing in the morning. If you can find something to smile about, do it and see how it changes your thoughts and your feelings.

An Interruption

One of the tools I use if I am getting overwhelmed by negative thoughts is a pattern interrupt. I visualise a stop sign. I actually have one in my coaching room on the wall. Another way to interrupt or change those negative emotions and thought patterns is to think about what that negative thought is. What triggers it? Give that negative thought a colour, sound or clarity so that you could describe it to someone if you had to. Visualise that thought as a shape, colour and give it a texture, rough or smooth, light or dark just use your imagination — whatever comes to you. Write that description down. Now shake it off and think of what you would like instead. For example, it could be that you feel you won't be able to present in front of the public successfully. You might make that fear of public speaking small, round, dark and hard. Write that down and then after you have 'broken state' or shaken that thought off, think of what you want, which would be the opposite. For example, it could be a love of public speaking and a sense of confidence and excitement. You could think of this as a squishy yellow cube (so in other words completely different to the fear. Then imagine you are looking at a TV screen and that small, round dark image is on the screen and your squishy yellow cube has shrunk down into the corner. Now make a sound 'swish' and accompany this with a hand movement as if you are swatting a fly and make that yellow cube big (or your description of what you *do* want). Make it huge and bright in front of you on the screen. You can even make a 'click' sound to lock it into place as it has overtaken the other image. This really does work, and you can use it for any image in your head or thought you would like to replace. This is much better than suppressing emotion. You can use this tool to interrupt the pattern you may have developed when emotions are triggered. Ruminating and habitually thinking negative thoughts can develop into a pattern, which in turn affects your personality and your life. It also affects relationships and has a much wider impact ecologically.

Teflon and Circles

Do you own any Teflon cookware? That coating helps everything slide off when you are cleaning up. There are many times when we are best to just let things 'slide.' If it still bothers you after a while, then do something about it. Many times you will find that what bothers you today may not even give you a second thought in the following week. Being an observer and having a sense of curiosity lightens these situations. Be curious about it and see if you think of it again the following week. Many times you will be surprised to notice that it hasn't cropped up again. After going through experiences in life, I have learned to be more discerning and not to implicitly trust everyone. We have circles around us and the people in our closest circle are those whom we know, trust and love. As the circles go outward, there are some people who are friends and close acquaintances and then there are others in another circle layer. This is all about taking notice. Being self-aware and aware of others is key.

Everyone Has a Story to Inspire and Learn From

Recently, I was at an International Women's Day Event held at a small art gallery. Artists and women from all walks of life, nationalities and cultures exhibited and gave short talks on their work. Helen Saba of Saba Real Estate spoke at the event, Helen was born in the Kurdistan province of Iran. Her childhood years were focused on survival during the Kurdistan and Iraq wars. She saw many things that children should not see. She escaped her country at age 19 under United Nations supervision, migrating to New Zealand with only $20 in her pocket and hardly speaking any English. She attended university, married and started a family. She always worked and studied at the same time. The family migrated to Australia, and unfortunately, her husband left her with two young children to support. She said that she had even less than the $20 she had started with when she arrived in New Zealand. She had to take petrol from the lawnmower to fuel the car to take the children to school. Her son had plastic bags over his socks to stop his feet from getting wet from the holes in his shoes. Through all the challenges and hardships, which included working seven days a week, she had a story about triumphing over her tribulations. She is now a top real estate agent who has received eight awards and is in the top 3 per cent of her industry. She went from being a mother who could not afford new shoes for her son to being able to buy him his favourite car for his twenty-first birthday. I love hearing stories like this! We can all learn from and be inspired by others.

Teddy's Gift

So, why is *Teddy's Revenge* such a good metaphor for life? It is because I believe dogs are special. Like children, dogs have the gift of taking each situation as it comes. They develop a kind of knowing about people and experiences. They don't hold grudges and they move on with the next part of their life.

I once read a clever explanation someone gave to their young son who was upset about their family dog passing away. The little boy asked his mother, 'Why do dogs die so much sooner than us?' The explanation given was that we all have lessons to learn during our life. She said, 'Dogs learn lessons a lot faster than humans and that is why during our lifetime we keep learning the lessons from many things that happen and many experiences so that we keep getting wiser and wiser. Dogs learn their lessons quickly and that is why a dog's life is much shorter than ours. They leave behind a special gift of memories to hold in our hearts which will make us smile when we think of them. We can also become wiser when we take notice of them and how they behave in certain circumstances.'

Commitment and Vision

My commitment is to be the best person I can for myself and my family. To Always do what I believe is the right thing. To trust my gut. To believe in myself and my abilities. To forgive myself and others. To love others where they are at and to realise that everyone is on their own personal journey. It is their journey and I have my own which will not exclude others that I love but rather run like parallel paths to theirs side by side, sometimes merging but always keeping the truth and values that are mine. To lead with integrity, honesty and respect. To be strong and keep boundaries intact on both sides with love and understanding. To be committed to those things consistently every day. To be strong and serve myself and others to the best of my ability.

My vision is to value add so that I can make a positive difference somewhere to someone every single day of my life. If every single person then did this then the world would be a better place. We can all value add with everything we do, endeavour to be the best we can be and encourage and support others to do the same.

The above was written in a notebook on 19 November 2010. After reading this again 12 years later, it is still my commitment and vision.

AFTERWORD

This book has provided a snapshot of my life. *Teddy's Revenge* was about a year when everything seemed to happen one event after another. As I was writing a book about my whole 61-plus years of life and everything that has happened in between, I realised that there is even more life to live. This snapshot encompasses everything that can happen in life, but in a different way. There will always be people who are worse off than you and those who are better off than you – financially, physically, emotionally, mentally and in every other aspect of life. One person's journey is never the same as another person's journey.

Everyone is fighting some kind of battle in their life, whether small or large and seemingly never-ending. I believe that life is so precious because of the highs and lows, the texture that dark and light times each bring. I hope that this book helps you to see that the joy is even more joyful because of sadness, and excitement is even more exciting because of disappointment. I never knew how much joy two little puppies could bring into life just as I never knew how much joy having children can bring. Life is rich and full of experiences to be had. I feel privileged and honoured to have experienced many aspects of life. Many of these I have not shared, however they are experiences that have shaped the person I am today. There are also many experiences I have not gone through, and I feel that by being aware and having empathy for others, I am learning along the way.

While writing this book over the last year, more world events have happened, including floods, earthquakes and the shocking war in Ukraine.

We just don't know what is around the corner in our own personal worlds, or the world as a whole. In our own individual ways, we deal with what we can however we can. I would like this book to be around as a snapshot of that time in my life, as well as a snapshot of a time when it feels as though the world has changed in so many ways.

Change is inevitable and happiness, joy and laughter are available if we can find ways to uncover those moments.

Life is made up of moments.

APPENDIX

Information on resources and further reading

For more on Moana's experience in Cyprus, go to AIMIS Healthcare Group's YouTube channel under Tarlov Cyst https://www.youtube.com/watch?v=X8x907LOvuY

To raise awareness and provide information for others who may be suffering, visit this article to read about the surgery Moana and two other Australians went through in 2015 This can be found on the Rare Disease Day website: https://www.rarediseaseday.org/stories/5452

Books and Resources

The Work by Byron Katie

https://thework.com/instruction-the-work-byron-katie/

mBraining by Grant Soosalu https://www.amazon.com.au/Mbraining-Using-Multiple-Brains-Stuff/dp/1475238584

Loving Your Life by Grant Soosalu is the book used for facilitating the *Loving Your Life in 30* which is available at Amazon and other good booksellers. https://www.amazon.com.au/Loving-Your-Life-Grant-Soosalu/dp/1517320569

Love 2.0 by Barbara Fredrickson

https://www.amazon.com/Love-2-0-Finding-Happiness-Connection/dp/0142180475

Viktor Emil Frankl (26 March 1905 – 2 September 1997)[1] was an Austrian neurologist, psychiatrist, philosopher, writer, and Holocaust survivor.[2] Frankl published 39 books.[5] The autobiographical *Man's Search for Meaning*, a best-selling book, is based on his experiences in various Nazi concentration camps.[6]

How Becoming a Coach Changed My Life by Glen Murdoch is available on Amazon and other bookstores or https://www.bstyledforlife.com.au/shop/

https://www.ted.com/speakers/amy_cuddy

https://www.ted.com/talks/moana_robinson_the_best_pieces_of_a_broken_world

B Styled for Life – Living with Sass and Style Over 50 by Moana Robinson is available on Amazon and other online bookstores or https://www.bstyledforlife.com.au/shop/

ACKNOWLEDGEMENTS

I am grateful to my family, friends and clients who have all been so thoughtful during difficult times in my life. Knowing that you have people who care makes getting through those times much easier.

I appreciate all the work doctors and nurses do, as well as the staff and vets at the animal emergency hospital and veterinary clinic.

Thank you to Helen Saba of Saba Real Estate who gave me permission to recount her story.

Thank you to the LYL mBIT Community and particularly the coaches I was working with during the time that we presented the *Loving Your Life in 30* sessions for attendees. Also thank you to my peer coaches who always have provided support and encouragement

Thank you especially to my husband, daughters, sons-in-law, grandchildren, mum and all of my family and friends.

Most of all, thank you, Teddy (and your little sister, Daisy) for coming into our lives and teaching us many of life's lessons.

ABOUT THE AUTHOR

As a businesswoman, wife, mother of two daughters and grandmother to six grandchildren, Moana feels blessed to have such a wonderful family. She enjoys life on the Gold Coast with her husband, Peter, after spending many years in Brisbane. She has two Cavoodles, Teddy and Daisy. Moana moved from New Zealand to Australia in 1986 with her husband just before the birth of their second daughter. Since then, her life has been interesting, challenging and rewarding. Moana has chosen to write this book as a legacy for her daughters and others to capture some challenges of the times, the lessons learned and wisdom gained as a reward. She hopes that others may be inspired to see many of life's challenges as opportunities to learn and gain even more self-awareness, which is the key to an exciting journey of discovery in life. Moana believes that true success comes from following your own path, connecting with people and discovering and using tools that empower you to think, feel and be all you can be. Moana has a business called B Styled for Life which is all about creating a life and style that is real and authentic to you. Moana believes that there is no better feeling than knowing who you are and what you stand for.

In the Polynesian language 'moana' means 'ocean'. Just as the ocean is integral to all life on Earth, Moana Robinson believes care and development of the mind, body and spirit are integral to us as individuals. Moana's goal as a qualified life coach and personal stylist is:

'To give each client the tools to have an awareness of the possibilities for their own unlimited potential in life and style.'

Moana shares that there is more to styling than just the outside image, inspiring people to develop their own resources to have **SASS** (Self Awareness and Self Sufficiency).

We have everything we need inside ourselves already to look, feel and be our absolute best.

Having **STYLE** is knowing who you are and expressing your unique personality. Wearing your best colours highlights your features and impacts how you see yourself and how others see you.

Moana enjoys motivating others through group presentations, whether online or in person, and can tailor talks and interactive sessions to suit your group or workplace. Moana holds workshops at clients' premises as well as at her studio. Workshops can include confidence building and styling sessions.

Moana's topics include but are not limited to:
- Stress Resilience Strategies
- Seven Steps to Style
- Show Your True Colours With Confidence
- Passion and Purpose After Changes in Life
- Uncover Your Style Workshops

Moana Robinson Dip.B.Th.
- +61 419 120 087
- moana@bstyledforlife.com.au
- www.bstyledforlife.com.au
- linktr.ee/BSFL

YOUR STRATEGY - YOUR TIPS - YOUR TOOLS

_____

_____

_____

_____

_____

_____

_____

_____

Teddy's Revenge

Your Strategy - Your Tips - Your Tools

Teddy's Revenge

Your Strategy - Your Tips - Your Tools

www.ingramcontent.com/pod-product-compliance
Lightning Source LLC
Chambersburg PA
CBHW030306100526
44590CB00012B/539